BEYOND ROOTS

II

If Anybody Ask You Who I Am

A Deeper Look at Blacks in the Bible

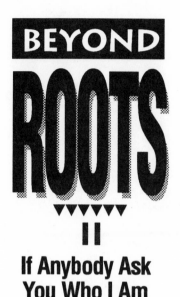

BEYOND ROOTS

II

If Anybody Ask You Who I Am

A Deeper Look at Blacks in the Bible

By

William Dwight McKissic, Sr.
and
Anthony T. Evans

RENAISSANCE PRODUCTIONS, INC.
601 MANTUA PIKE, SUITE 200
WENONAH, NJ 08090
1-800-234-2338

Published by
RENAISSANCE PRODUCTIONS, INC.
601 Mantua Pike, Suite 200
Wenonah, New Jersey 08090
1-800-234-2338

© 1994 by William Dwight McKissic
        and Anthony T. Evans

ISBN #0-9625605-5-3

Unless otherwise noted, Scripture quotations
are taken from the King James Version of the
Holy Bible and the New American Standard Bible,
© 1960, 1963, 1968, 1971, 1972, 1973, 1975, and
1977 by the Lockman Foundation.

Printed in the United States of America
94 95 96 97 98 99/10 9 8 7 6 5 4 3 2

CONTENTS

ACKNOWLEDGEMENTS

A work such as this is not accomplished without the assistance and expertise of others. We owe a great deal of gratitude to Mrs. Gloria Ford and Mrs. Linda Fitzgerald who typed the manuscript; Mrs. Sylvia Vittatoe who compiled the manuscript and put it into its final form; and Rev. Richard Greene and Rev. Bob Tower who provided qualitative research assistance.

We also want to express a special word of thanks to our wives, Vera McKissic and Lois Evans, for their patience, understanding and faithful support during the preparation of this manuscript.

These technically excellent and spiritually mature persons clearly reflect the continual legacy of God's activity in people of African descent.

FOREWORD

Beyond Roots II is the logical second step in the cultural literary pilgrimage of both Rev. McKissic and Dr. Evans. As two bibliocentric evangelical African American Pastors, they seek to flush out the errors in the biblical interpretations of the history of the Black race in a scholarly and pragmatic way. McKissic and Evans are determined to continue their wrestlings until they can penetrate the truth about a significant Black presence in the Bible, not only in the African American community, but for the benefit of the Christian church at large.

In Beyond Roots I, Rev. McKissic clearly proves the case that the Black presence in the Bible is unmistakably clear. It unearths the treasures of Scripture regarding God's intentional creation, identification and dissemination of African people throughout the biblical world. His work makes it clear that people of African descent are not a mere afterthought of God, and that their presence in Scripture, by His design, is both comprehensive and strategic.

In Dr. Evans' work, Are Blacks Spiritually Inferior To Whites?: The Dispelling of an American Myth, he argues that the Black church, during slavery, is probably the greatest demonstration of biblical Christianity in the history of America. His passion was to dispel the myth of spiritual inferiority that has allowed whites to ignore the biblical and historical contributions of Black Christians. He also challenges the Black church to "go back to the future" to recapture the influence, impact and comprehensive biblical world view which once defined the Black church and made it the epicenter of all of Black life.

In this collaborative work, McKissic and Evans fill in the gaps between their works to show why a proper biblical view of the Black race is essential if Black people are to recognize, understand and appreciate their position in God's eternal program. This work further authenticates the Black presence in Scripture through the eyes of Black and White biblical scholars while pointing to the racial abuse of historically accepted biblical scholarship. In addition, they reveal the continuing Black presence in the development of the church and theology through the leadership of the African church fathers and beyond. However, this work is designed not only to unfold the divine saga of the Black race in Scripture, but to make an analysis of how people must use that knowledge to address the contemporary crisis that African Americans currently face. It is designed to challenge Black and White Christians alike to root their racial heritage and pride in Scripture if they are to avoid the extremes of both racial elitism or racial inferiority.

Renaissance Productions hopes that this work will further contribute to the "inspired" new wave of Christian African-American writers who are seeking to use the Bible to answer the questions of identity that continues to haunt people of African-American descent. It is the contention of both Evans and McKissic that true and authentic racial and cultural identity can only be found in God and His written word, the Bible. We believe that true racial and cultural identity can only be found in God and His written word, the Bible. Only when Christians understand the beauty of biblically based racial diversity, and see its integration into the saga of divine unity, will the world truly know that Jesus is indeed the Christ, Son of the living God.

Roland G. Hardy, Jr.
President
Renaissance Productions, Inc.

Chapter 1

THE HEART OF THE MATTER

This book represents the efforts of two African-American evangelical brothers to discover and disseminate information about our ancestors in biblical anthropology and early Christian history in order to address an area of interest that is seldom addressed in colleges, seminaries and churches. It is also our goal to provide answers to many who raise questions regarding our race and our faith. Why is it important that we trace our biblical and early Christian history ancestry? Identity and definition are probably the two most important contributing factors to success in life. WHO AM I?–WHERE DID I COME FROM?–WHY AM I HERE?– WHERE AM I GOING?–are questions each of us ask ourselves that must be ultimately answered from the Bible, reliable historical and technical information, and our relationship with God.

There is a growing awareness toward the acknowledgement of our glorious African heritage, which many heretofore have viewed as information left only to a select few. It is not enough that scholars dig up to record and academically teach the wonderful facts of God's scarlet thread of grace that has historically run through people of African descent. Unless this knowledge trickles down to "Aunt Jane" and "Deacon Jones", then it will be of little use to the masses who are in desperate need of God's truth about who we are. These glorious truths must be used for a resurgence of identity which will enable us to appropriately address our contemporary situation.

African Americans are currently undergoing an identity crisis of serious proportions. Our own self-consciousness is at a level of vulnerability. Some in the Afro-centric movement, on one hand, seeks to make everything a Black issue, while on the other hand, there are those who wish to function in a sphere of racial neutrality, as though Africa and Africans had no part in the outworking of God's eternal plan. This cultural ambiguity has opened the door for theological and cultural movements, all seeking primarily one thing, the souls of Black folks.

This identity crisis is seen in the frustrated attempts of the Black middle class to relate to the Black underclass. As the crisis of class within the African American community competes with the crisis of racism within the Anglo community, the crisis of identity becomes more complex. This crisis further betrays and undermines the civil rights agenda as well as the Black Democratic political establishment. Both sides claim to be the authentic representative of the poor and disenfranchised black masses. The crisis is also graphically portrayed in the tragic black on black violence in the African American community throughout the country. The unimaginable reality of considering the National Guard to maintain order in our Nation's capital is testimony to the extent of the crisis. When Black's randomly kill our own without even the slightest prick of conscience, the lack of self respect and racial respect which we once knew as people is evident.

In the midst of the crisis the Black church attempts to clarify its contemporary role as the guardian of Black life. But due to a lack of clarity, the door has been opened to Islamic convictions within the Christian community. It is not unusual to see a host of black ministers on the same platform with Louis Farrakhan listening and affirming him as he speaks equally authoritatively on both the Bible and the Koran.

It is for this very reason that there must be a new awakening among Christian African Americans who are rooted in the "faith of our fathers." The contemporary need is for a view of ethnicity that is not limited to the transitory movements, philosophies and whims of men. The need is not for more racial pride programs, but rather for a lasting standardized approach to racial authenticity that transcends the ever-changing Black consciousness which engulfs us. Our primary concern should be what God's Word affirms about us, not the word of self-appointed Black or White leadership. Unless Black identity is rooted in biblical identity, we may very well wind up with a false identity or, even worse, no identity at all, as our contemporary situation currently reflects. It should be apparent that our needs go beyond simply voting for more politicians. Our situation continues to decline in spite of an abundance of political leaders.

Our crisis also goes beyond blaming racism since racism is not the reason Black men impregnate our teenage girls while abandoning their offspring. Racism is not the reason homicide is the number one cause of death for Black men between the ages of 15 and 25 years of age. Racism is not forcing the middle class to abandon the underclass. Could it be, that a large part of our problem is that we have become a people who have forgotten who we are? Our loss of identity has made us vulnerable to foreign identities which instead of liberating us have further enslaved us. It has enslaved us to ourselves -- and self-induced slavery is the worse type of bondage.

Racism has left an indelible mark on the Black psyche and has created a climate which exasperates our own self-analysis. However, we must never succumb to its influence. Racism has been around for a long time, and as is apparent, will not disappear in the near future. While racism must be addressed and fought, it cannot be allowed to prevent us from doing what is necessary to get our own house in order. We must determine what our community would be if racism did not exist, and then move forward in building such a community. This can only exist from a bibliocentric point of view.

Reclaiming the Black Family

It is our contention that because of a biblical identity rooted in the God of the Bible, our forefathers were able to not only survive slavery, but progress as a people in spite of it. Taking their cue from the Old Testament, black neighborhoods functioned like extended families. Almost everyone you knew was like an aunt, uncle or cousin. The elderly were treated with the utmost respect, and everyone held everyone else accountable for proper behavior. Bearing and raising children were viewed as a great goal and privilege, and marriage was held in the highest esteem. In spite of slavery, Jim Crow, and segregation we were able to foster family, community, and black civilization. This is only explainable by the existence of a self-consciousness that permeated our race. Our children were cared for because our forefathers understood they bore the image of God. In fact, the reason that we, as a people, did not succumb to the travesty of slavery is that the image of God was culturally impressed upon us collectively. We had a theocratic world-view.

There is no place more strategic to provide a theocratic world-view than in the family. It is for this very reason that there can be no authentic Black identity unless we reclaim our Black families. Unless we pass on the strengths of our God-given heritage to the next generation, we can never hope to see true, lasting change take place in our community.

As parents we are to teach our children to fight back against racism intellectually rather than physically. The result of such tutorship was evident when Dwight and J.E. McKissic, sons of the co-author, knew exactly how to reeducate their peers. During a game of basketball with their neighbors they were accosted after winning several games when one child shouted 'You may be better than us at basketball but Whites are smarter than Blacks!' To which Dwight and J.E. responded, 'We are descendants of the ancient Egyptians and the ancient Mesopotamians (Sumerians) and our people enslaved your people before your people enslaved us.' That was the true victory of the competition!

We have to give our children the moral and spiritual foundation with which they can--and will want to--reject the negative values thrust upon them. That means first and foremost, we along with our children must attend churches that teach the Bible and are Christ-centered as well as culturally cognizant. Unless we demonstrate the importance of the church in the life of the family, our kids will not know the truth and the tragic result will be that others will shape and mold their identity.

Our foreparents did not have access to family seminars and the newest Christian literature. In those years, blacks were rarely included in major Christian outreaches. But they did have the Bible, a passionate love for Jesus Christ, each other, and their children, and somehow that was enough. By this we have sufficient proof that economic, racial and class limitations need not be the last word in the way our children lead their lives.

We have too rich a heritage with too great a God to have the kind of disintegration among our children we are now experiencing. It will take every ounce of our energy to reclaim our families. But if not now, when? And if not us, who?

The Role of the Church

The primary reason Blacks remained sane during the worst of times was due to the role of the church as the guardian of our collective identity under God. As the center of community life, the church kept us from allowing either the social situation of slavery or the culture from determining our identity or existence. It made us understand that God, and only God, was the one who defined our humanity and destiny. The Black church taught us weekly and empowered the black family to remind us daily of our divine heritage and bibliocentric identity. The church taught barefoot black boys, "I got shoes, you got shoes, all God's children got shoes." The church taught the fatherless that God was their new Father. The church taught the sick that there was a "Balm in Gilead." The church taught those in trouble that God was a lawyer in the courtroom and "a very present help in the time of trouble." In other words, God was "our all in all."

This world-view, however, was not mere serendipity without a tangible reality. The Black church, in slavery, was the greatest expression of comprehensive biblical Christianity in the history of America because it was able to merge truth with practice. It did it in such a natural way that Blacks saw their identity expressed and reinforced in being part of the community. Serving as the citadel and focal point of all of Black life, the historical Black church gave birth to the black press, educational institutions, sociopolitical movements, financial institutions and surrogate families. What is so staggering is that these accomplishments were made during a time when there were no government grants, welfare systems or anti-poverty programs. If Black America is to deliver itself from its misguided identity, then the Black church must once again serve as the source of our identity under God.

If Anybody Asks You

The title of the book was borrowed from a familiar song sang in Black churches by the same name "If anybody ask you who I am." At the heart of the song is the issue of identity. It is our contention that every Black evangelical Christian ought to be prepared and able to answer the following questions if anybody ask them who they are: What Bible character had three descendants, one of which settled on African soil? Where was the garden of Eden? Who was the father of darkest complexioned people in Scripture? How did Ham get his complexion? Were Blacks ever cursed in Scripture? What role did Africans play in the New Testament and post--New Testament Christianity? What color was Jesus? What was the role and identity of the Black man in ancient biblical history? To a great degree we have by default delegated the answers to these crucial questions to the majority culture. It is time to lay the axe at the root of the tree and chop down all the ambiguous, unbiblical, self serving, historically inaccurate and demeaning answers that we have been given.

It is unmistakable in African history, Black American history, church history, and contemporary scholastic analysis that God has intimately and strategically woven the black presence into His redemptive program. Unfortunately, some scholars have chosen to subvert, manipulate and passively ignore this fact in order to maintain an ethic of racial superiority and cultural elitism. Conversely, others have taken those truths as a basis for deifying blackness. Both extremes are sin because they seek to ethnologize God. Such a racially expedient God cannot be the true God of the Bible.

It is the intention of this work to exhibit Scripture and its supporting historical documentation as ammunition to give Blacks our rightful due as a strategic and intricate part in God's divine plan. Furthermore, it is our contention that the pride of Blacks, or any people for that matter, ought to be only rooted in that which the Bible authenticates. Failure to do so opens up a "Pandora's Box" of cultural and racial fluidity. This will allow one of any race to subvert the truth in order to subjugate their fellowman and misrepresent the intentions of God in history. The repercussions of such misrepresentation can be staggering, as American slavery and South African apartheid clearly reveals.

This book then, is not just about definition and identification, history and exegesis, afrocentrism or early African Christian history. This book is written to help Black people look beyond race and see the justice and righteousness of God, who shows partiality to no one (Acts 10:34). This book is written to lead men and women to faith in Jesus Christ, who is not willing that any should perish but that all should come to repentance (2 Peter 3:9).

This book is also written to help our White brothers and sisters understand how we view ourselves in biblical and early church history so that they will not view us as "Johnny Come Latelys" on the scene of Christian world history, or as an aberration in the plan of God. Rather, we should be seen as descendants of Noah through Ham, just as our White brothers are descendants of Noah through Japheth, and our Jewish and Arabic (Semitic) brothers are descendants of Noah through Shem. We challenge our White brothers to teach the richness of our Hamitic heritage since it is part of the whole council of God. The inevitable result of such comprehensive Christian education will be the realization of the dream of seeing Black and White Christians coming together biblically and cooperatively to once and for all address the issue of race and the sin of racism. Once and for all we will be able to jointly model the scriptural admonitions for racial justice, equality and unity (Malachi 2:10; Amos 9:7; Mark 3:22-25; Acts 10:34, 17:26; Galatians 3:28; Revelation 5:9, etc.). Furthermore we will together be able to repudiate all of the false teaching done in the name of Christianity that has and is polarizing the experiencing of our oneness in Christ.

When Christians of any race decide to recognize the Bible's answer to the question of ethnicity, a progression of healing, understanding and tolerance becomes the natural and automatic result. On the other hand, when we leave the racial critique to those who use and misuse divine revelation for their own selfish purposes, the result is always dehumanization, oppression, intolerance and pride; the things that incite the wrath of God!

It is time for all people to recognize that the Divine saga is inclusive of all races since His earthly program is represented by every nation, kindred, tribe and tongue (Rev. 7:9). It is time for us to recognize that unless our individual or group colors are red, representing the precious blood of Jesus Christ, then whatever culture, race or class we represent becomes temporarily and eternally cursed. Our oneness in Jesus Christ should serve as the basis and criteria by which we judge and evaluate the accepted standards of our own ethnicity and the ethnicity of others. Only in this way can we arrive at Christian unity and cooperation that Christ so deeply desires for His people to share. Only as our unity, cross-racially and cross-culturally, is manifested to the world can people see the reality of the living Christ as magnified through His wonderful multicolored race of people.

What then is the heart of the matter? "Black is only truly beautiful if its biblical, and white is only right if it agrees with Holy Writ". So, by the end of this book, if anyone asks you who we are, tell them we are not products of the mark of Cain, or the curse of Ham. Tell them we are not the product of the dispersion after the Tower of Babel or coincidental environmental factors. If anybody ask you tell them we are not products of a strange diet, neither did we descend from apes or monkeys. If anybody ask you tell them WE ARE sons of the soil, descendants from Adam who was a product of African ground (Genesis 2:7,13). Tell them we descended from Ham, whose descendants even in their day had a nose like ours, lips like ours, hair like ours and a complexion like ours. If anybody ask you tell them that through the Coptic Church and African Church fathers we made great contributions to the development and expansion of the Christian faith prior to slavery in America. If anybody ask you who we are and you can't remember Hamite, Cushite, Canaanite, Ethiopian, African, Negro, people of color, or Moor; tell them there is a designation we prefer above all these. Tell them the same thing that the Negro spiritual says. Tell them we are children of the King. Before you tell them of the glory of our African past; before you broadcast on the splendor of our historical roots; before you wax eloquent on the contributions of our ancestors and before you exegete the intricate excellencies of our racial stock, you must first shout from the rooftops that we are Christians, followers of the Lord Jesus Christ who loved us and gave Himself for us on Calvary's cross. He alone is the One whose name is above every name; the One at whose name "every knee will bow and every tongue confess", regardless of history, culture, class or background. When all is said and done, the only name that will matter is the name Jesus Christ and the only family that will count will be the family of God. Irrespective of how history has treated us—we belong to the family of God. Irrespective of how we have treated ourselves, through the blood of Christ, we've been sanctified. For only as our racial identity and culture is rooted in Him will it have ultimate meaning and purpose.

Chapter 2

THE TRUTH DENIED

The intention of this study is not to accuse anyone of being racist. Our purpose is to focus on various viewpoints--most of which are misinformed, fallacious and inconsiderate to the Black race--held particularly by White biblical commentators. Conversely, our purpose is to direct the attention of Blacks to critically think through the issues for themselves, and not to rely solely on Whites to inform us about our ancient and biblical history.

From the study of Genesis, we have concluded that Noah's son, Ham, was Black. Biblical commentaries and dictionaries that were consulted did not address the question with a consistent voice. There were neither clear nor consistent answers given regarding the ethnicity of Ham, the ethnicity of Ham's descendants or the etymology of Ham. We did notice, nonetheless, that there was consistency regarding the etymology and ethnicity of Japheth, Shem and their descendants, but not Ham. Dr. William Elder who received his Ph.D. in the Old Testament from Baylor University was consulted. He was first asked whether Ham was Black. Dr. Elder replied that the opinion held by the most respected Old Testament scholars was that Ham was indeed Black. Then, the Canaanites came into question; and the assumption of conversation was that the Canaanites were Black. It was at that time Dr. Elder interrupted and said, "But the Canaanites were White." Then the counter-argument was that if Ham was Black and Canaan was his son, how could the Canaanites be White?" Then Dr. Elder responded: "I believe that is right."

Dr. Elder, like most conservative evangelical scholars had not thought through the implications of Ham's Black heritage. According to Rev. Stan Harris, a graduate of Hyles-Anderson College, Indiana, most independent fundamental colleges teach that Blacks descended from Ham who was cursed and therefore, Blacks are cursed.[1] Consequently, most students graduate from evangelical and fundamental colleges with a fabricated or unclear view of Ham and his descendants. They are taught that Ham was the progenitor of the Black race and was cursed by Noah.

An alumnus of a well known Southern conservative Bible college shared that all students were required to take a test that included these two questions: Who was the biblical father of the Caucasian/Indo European people? Who was the biblical father of the Jewish and Arabic people? But there was no question asked regarding who was the biblical father of the African or Negroid people. This alumnus said the test left him with the feeling that Blacks had no biblical heritage.[2] Not only are most schools ambivalent and apathetic regarding this issue, but most biblical dictionaries, commentaries and encyclopedias treat the subject with the same distance as the schools.

The International Standard Bible Encyclopedia (ISBE), first published in 1915, has long been considered a standard among biblical reference works. The following comments were made concerning Africa:

> In the Table of Nations (Gen.10) the sons of Ham are named: Cush, Egypt (or Mizram), Put, and Canaan (10:7). Except for Canaan, whose descendants (10:15-19) occupied the eastern coastlands of the Mediterranean, these are generally located in Africa... It is evident that all of the peoples who can be identified as "African" are Caucasoid. There are no nations mentioned that can be identified anthropologically as Negroid. The Nubians, and for that matter, the Ethiopians, while black-skinned, do not fit the anthropological description of the Negroes... We can only conclude that the Bible limits its references to the peoples of the Eastern Mediterranean and adjacent areas; and so far as Africa is concerned, this means North Africa and the Nile Valley to Nubia. [3]

It is almost unbelievable that ISBE could claim that, "...All of the people who can be identified as 'African' are Caucasoid." ISBE maintains that "African" refers to the sons of Ham who settled in "North Africa and the Nile Valley to Nubia" and during the biblical period they were considered 'Caucasoid'. Conversely, ISBE describes the Nubians and Ethiopians as "black-skinned."[4] Alongside the commentary is a picture of "wooden figures of Nubian bowmen" (2050-1800 B.C. from Siut), providing without doubt that black-skinned men with afro hairstyles are not Caucasoid by appellation.

The only way that ISBE can justify that the Nubians and Ethiopians were "Caucasoid" is if they employed the broad definition for "Caucasoid" similar to the one listed in The Grolier Encyclopedia:

> Caucasoid: One of the major groups of mankind, skin color varies from white to dark brown. Head hair is usually wavy, but varies from silky straight to various degrees of curliness. It is almost never wooly, rarely frizzy, and is seldom as thick in the individual hairs or as sparsely distributed as in Mongoloids....The Caucasoid major group is often called 'white.' This is incorrect because the group includes many peoples of dark skin color, such as the Australian aborigines, the Veddahs of Ceylon, and the pre-Dravidians of central and southern India... Representative

Caucasoid ethnic groups are the Mediterranean, Atlanto-Mediterranean, Irano-Afghan, Alpine, Dinaric, Armenoid, Hamitic, East Baltic, Indo Dravidian, and Polynesian. [5]

This definition for "Caucasoid" allows unsuspecting biblical scholars to label anyone as Caucasian, while excluding others who would meet the same criteria. This broad definition of Caucasoid has caused us to be cautious when biblical characters and countries are labeled "Caucasoid or Caucasian", unless of course, there is supporting evidence or logic which dictates such a designation.

It is obvious that much of the history of the Black race has been scholastically robbed from us by employing such broad definitions of Caucasoid (Caucasian) as recorded by ISBE and Grolier.

Mostafa Hefney, an Egyptian, indicated in *Jet Magazine* recently, "My complexion is as dark as most Black Americans. My features are clearly African." [6] But since he is a naturalized citizen of Egypt, the U.S. Department of Immigration, Directive Number 15, classifies him as White. Hefney adds, "Classification as it is done by the United States Government provides Whites with legal ground to claim Egypt as a White civilization. We are fools if we allow them to take this legacy from us." [7] We obviously agree with Hefney.

If Nubians or Ethiopians, as described and pictured by ISBE, were to have mug photographs taken in America, there would be no question that they would be classified as Black. Also, if they had attempted to buy a cup of coffee in Georgia, Alabama, Mississippi, or Arkansas in a White restaurant during the first half of this century, they would have been denied access because they were Negro or Colored. Yet, black-skinned, `wooly hair' people in selective places in Africa and the Middle East are "anthropologically" classified as Caucasians. Some biblical scholars go so far as to label North Africa and the Nile Valley area as "Euro-Africa." [8] ISBE labels the Canaanites "Caucasoid"[9] and the "Cushite woman" Moses married as "probably implying a dark skinned Egyptian, descendant of the Nubians."[10]

The denial of the Negro heritage from Ham is consistently upheld. *The Pictorial Bible Dictionary* records that Ham "became the progenitor of the dark races; not the Negroes, but the Egyptians, Ethiopians, Libyans and Canaanites."[11] *The New Compact Bible Dictionary* states Ham became the progenitor of the dark races, not the Negroes, but the Egyptians, Libyans and Canaanites (Gen. 10:6-20).[12] *The Living Bible* states, "Ham was not the ancestor of the Negro, as was once erroneously supposed."[13] *Webster's Student Dictionary* defines a Hamite as "A Caucasian of the chief native race of North Africa."[14] T.B. Matson commented with regard to the ethnicity and etymology of Ham and Hamites:

The Negro is not a descendant of Canaan. He may have come from the line of Cush, although some scholars claim he is not a Hamite at all... Some have assumed that the Negro got his color from his father, Ham, since the latter could mean "dark" or "black." However, Ham could also mean "warm" or "hot." If so, it could also refer to the warm or hot climate where the Hamites lived. If it meant "black or dark," it could refer to the black soil in the Nile Valley, where so many of the children of Ham settled. 'It is unnecessary to conclude that the meaning of Ham's name refers to the color of any of his descendants or that it suggests that the curse includes all people who have black skin.' [15]

Matson seems to agree with the position that the Negro is a descendant of Ham. However, he rejects the notion that the Negro was a descendant of Canaan, implying that he may have descended from the Cush.

Cush was the brother of Canaan and the son of Ham. On a hieroglyphic from an Egyptian tomb circa fourteenth century B.C., some ancient artists depicted several races of people in a queue where the Cushites were depicted as black-skinned; the "Asiatics," or Canaanites, as dark brown, and the Egyptians as a reddish brown.[16] The Cushites, Canaanites and Egyptians are all descendants of Ham and archaeology proves that they were of dark complexions. We are baffled and grieved that some commentators refuse to acknowledge all Hamites as Negroes. If the Black race did not descend from Ham, Cush, Mizraim, Phut and Canaan (Gen. 10:6) then who is the forefather of the Negro? Those who argue that Ham and his descendants were not Black have failed to produce evidence to support their thesis.

Biblical commentators do not deny that the Greeks, Romans, and Germans (Europeans) can trace their origin to Japheth (Gen. 10:1-5). Neither do they deny or argue against the fact that the Jews and Arabs can trace their origin to Shem (Gen. 10:21-32). However, there is much debate on whether Negroes are the descendants of Ham.

Some White scholars are of the opinion that the descendants of Ham are black because of the climate. This theory is readily used to justify the dark complexion of the Negro. If Blacks are dark solely due to the climate, that would mean we are Black by coincidence and not by Divine intent. When Noah named his sons "Ham" meaning "dark or black," "Shem" meaning dusky or olive colored" and "Japheth" meaning bright or fair, either physically or prophetically, he based their names from visual observation of their range of skin colors.

ISBE denies the Hamites (Gen. 10:6) were Negroes, yet maintains that, "recent studies of African history reveal the existence in central Africa of a high level of civilization, probably nurtured by the posterity of Ham."[17]   We wonder if the ISBE authors presume that such a "high level of civilization" in Central Africa was built due to the presence of the Caucasoid and not the Negro. If that is so, then they have not only taken North and East Africa from Blacks but also Central Africa. On the other hand, if they considered the central African people to be of the posterity of Ham which is Black or Negroid people, how can they deny that the North and East African people who were descendants of Ham were not also Black?

Dr. Clem Davies, in his book, *The Racial Streams of Mankind* demonstrated the intellectual confusion that typifies discussion of Ham and Black people in Scripture. In chapter 1 entitled "The Three Streams" he wrote:

> The Hamitic stream is identified with the African, partly with the Indian, and partly with the Chinese....Ham was not a colored person. To begin with, the Egyptians were children of Ham, most of the Egyptians anyway; they were swarthy but not black....Ham was the father of the African people and of the main body of the people of India....the Hamites are found today in the dark races of the world, the backward races. We speak of 'darkest Africa', and it is "dark" in more senses than one, for it was in this section of the globe that the offspring of Ham have been most prolific.[18]

First of all, Davies recorded that "the Hamitic stream is identified with the African people."[19] But, in his first chapter he made it clear that Ham "was not a colored person." One would naturally assume that if Ham was not a "colored person" then he must have been a White person. Nevertheless, he claimed the Hamites are found today in the dark races of the world. In chapter 2, although he related Egypt to Ham, he maintained that as the Hamites moved into inner Africa they became "darker" spiritually, intellectually, and physically. Davies specified:

> Thus Ham became the father of the Egyptians, the early Chaldees, and the Canaanites, His descendants journeyed deeply into Africa, and the deeper they went, the less became their wisdom. They became beings between men and brutes; their very souls and brains were different. They were not 'men of like passions as we are,' and finally even their very dialects - the most meager and monosyllabic of all the original speech were lost. They became ugly and degraded. You have only to witness the films shown today of the natives of 'darkest Africa' to see to what depths the Hamitic strain has descended to an utterable mental and spiritual darkness, the veritable nadir of civilization.[20]

The confusion continued on the sixtieth page of Davies book where he stated, "From Phut came all the Negroid races, spreading across to Libya and down into dark Africa." Phut was Ham's son and according to Davies the progenitor of the Negro race. In regard to Cush, the chapter entitled "*The Line of Ham*", Davis reported:

> For four thousand years the children of Cush, one of the sons of Ham, wandered over the torrid plains and countries of Africa. They lived as savages then, and they are savages today. [21]

It is because of mistaken commentators like Davies that we find it necessary to refute their precise arguments to set the record straight. It almost goes without saying that Davies believed that the Hamites were an "accursed" race. Davies offers no supporting evidence that the children of Cush were "savages." Neither does he offer ethnological data that shows how "from Phut came all the Negroid races." Phut was a son of Ham, yet "Ham was not a colored person." [22]

Davies also agreed to the climatic viewpoint regarding the origin of Black people:

> ...a person's color is determined by his nearness to, or distance from the sun. If the black people lived long enough in northern climates, over a space of several thousand years their skin might become white. [23]

The Black Colchians of Russia whom Herodotus described as "black skin and wooly hair"[24] have lived in Russia for several thousand years and they are yet to turn White, neither have the Black Eskimos near the North Pole.

The Keil And Delitzsch Commentary on the Old Testament, a critical commentary by German scholars, is a respected and a popular reference source in American ecclesiastical circles. Similar to Davies, but in a more subtle manner, Keil and Delitzsch also embraced the curse of Ham:

> In the sin of Ham there lies the great stain of the whole Hamitic race, whose chief characteristic is sexual sin; and the curse which Noah pronounce upon this sin still rests upon the race... Although this curse was announced upon Canaan alone, the fact that Ham had no share in Noah's blessing, either for himself or his other sons, was sufficient proof that his whole family was included by implication in the curse, even if it was to fall chiefly upon Canaan. And history confirms the supposition. The Canaanites were

partly exterminated, and partly subjected to the lowest form of slavery, by the Israelites, who belonged to the family of Shem; and those who still remained were reduced by Solomon to the same condition, (I Kings 9,20,21). The Phonecians, along with the Carthaginians and the Egyptians, who all belonged to the family of Canaan, were subjected by the Japhetic Persians, Macedonians, and Romans; and the remainder of the Hamitic tribes either shared the same fate, or still sigh, like the Negroes, for example, and other African tribes, beneath the yoke of the most crushing slavery. [25]

Later we respond to Keil-Delitzsch interpretation of the "curse of Ham". However, suffice it to say at this point, we are extremely thankful that Keil and Delitzsch considered the Hamites Negroes and linked the Phoenicians, Carthaginians, Egyptians and Canaanites with the "Negroes...and other African tribes." Keil and Delitzsch also made it clear that they regarded the dark complexion of the Egyptians to be indicative of their Hamitic descent. [26]

In the *Hebrew - English Edition of the Babylonian Talmud* is recorded one of the earlier extra-biblical references to the "curse of Ham": "Our Rabbis taught: 'Three copulated in the ark, and they were all punished - the dog, the raven, and Ham. The dog was doom to be tied, the raven expectorates [his seed into his mate's mouth] and Ham was smitten in his skin.'" The explanatory footnote states..."from him [Ham] descended Cush (the negro who is black skinned). [27]

Dr. Thomas Virgil Peterson in his book *Ham and Japheth*, shared insights from the Jewish Midrashim (folk stories and legends) collected in the Babylonian Talmud between A.D. 200 and 600. These insights can also be found in other writings before A.D. 1000. The Negro's blackness and slavery which resulted from Noah's curse, was first suggested in the Jewish Midrashim. It described Ham's sin as having been a filial disrespect, castration, sexual abuse, or illicit sex on the ark. "The Jewish legends identified Ham as the father of the Negro race" [28] according to Peterson.

The Bereshith Rabbah, an expository commentary on Genesis utilizing the work of Rabis from the second to fourth centuries, alluded to the tradition that Ham castrated Noah. The Rabbi Joseph imagined a conversation between Noah and Ham:

You have prevented me from doing something in the dark (cohabitation) therefore your seed will be ugly and dark skinned. The descendants of Ham through Canaan have red eyes, because Ham looked upon the nakedness of his father; they have mishappen lips, because Ham spoke with his lips to his brothers about the unseemly condition of his father; they have twisted curly hair, because Ham turned and twisted his head around to see the nakedness of his father; and they go about naked, because Ham did not cover the nakedness of his father. [29]

Although the above comments recorded in the Babylonian Talmud are obviously isogenous, they are erroneously inconsiderate. Nevertheless we find it interesting that the Jewish Rabbis, from A.D. 200 and 1000, considered the descendants of Ham unquestionably to be Negroes. In contrast many modern scholars, 1000 years removed from that era, are reluctant to classify the Hamites as Negroes. Admittedly, the Rabbis were bias toward people of Hamitic descent, but they provided a marvelous testimony of the fact that people of Hamitic descent were Negroes.

Augustine Calmet, a French Benedictine abbot of Senones published a four volume dictionary in 1722-1728 in Paris entitled *Dictionary Of The Holy Bible*. In his dictionary Calmet translated the name "Ham" as "burnt" "swarthy" and "black" and maintained that when Noah cursed Ham his skin became black and he gave Noah Africa for his inheritance. Calmet wrote, "that Noah having cursed Ham and Canaan, the effect was, that not only their posterity became subject to their brethren, and was born, as we may say, in slavery, but likewise that the color of their skin suddenly became black." [30]

Responding to Calmet's position that Ham "suddenly became black," Thomas Peterson argued,..."since etymology of the word Ham provided the principle proof that Ham was black, he must have been black when he entered the ark." [31] While reading Peterson's book we discovered that Calmet was quoted by several supporters of slavery during that era in America. He taught that Noah cursed Ham and Canaan. The Scripture says "Cursed be Canaan" (Gen. 9:25 KJV). Unfortunately, men trusted the word of Calmet over the word of Christ and approvingly quoted him.

Just for the record, such well known Bible commentators as C. I. Scofield [32], Arthur Pink [33], and Jamieson, Fausett, and Brown [34] have embraced and endorsed in their writings the "curse of Ham" theory. Again, we are glad that these men acknowledged a Black presence in Scripture. Unfortunately, they basically limited their discussion of Ham and his descendants to the "infamous" passage in Genesis 9.

The old *Scofield Reference Bible*, one of the most influential reference works revered by the Evangelical Fundamentalist community, became the harbinger of disinformation against dark-skinned peoples, generally thought to be the descendants of Ham. In his note on the descendents of Noah's three sons in Genesis 9, Scofield remarked, "A prophetic declaration is made that from Ham will descend an inferior and servile posterity (Gen. 9.24, 25). [35] "In addition to being incorrect, comments such as Scofield's gave full consent to nourish the notion of a biblically sanctioned Black inferiority. This comment did nothing to ameliorate the already culturally inflicted and discolored perception of Black people in the minds of White Bible students. It is unfortunate for both Blacks and Whites alike that this footnote would fall before the eyes of so many readers in light of the Scofield Reference Bible's 'inspired' popularity in Fundamentalist camps.

As Ernest R. Sandeen states in his book *The Roots of Fundamentalism*, "The Bible [Scofield Reference Bible]...is perhaps the most influential single publication in millenarian and Fundamental historiography."[36] Although his Reference Bible was influential in one sense, Scofield's note became infamous to all of the descendants of Ham, even though Noah's curse was correctly and verifiably confined to Canaan. "Cursed be Canaan; A servant of servants He shall be to his brothers" (Gen. 9:25). It is true that from Ham came a people who would be servants to the descendents of the other sons of Noah; however, it is not the entire truth. In Genesis 10, Moses further delineates the geneology of Ham. It is noteworthy that Moses, the author, does not at all impute Canaan's servility to the other siblings of Ham; Cush, Put and Mizraim. In fact Nimrod, the son of Cush, was said to have become " a mighty one on the earth" (Gen. 10:8) and was also the progenitor of two of the greatest cities of antiquity, Nineveh and Babel, two cities which hardly could be characterized as servile or lacking in military wherewithal. Obviously Scofield's brief footnote lacked some vital detail and thus fostered faulty fallacies associating servility and inferiority to blackness. We can take heart that in later versions of the Schofield Reference Bible the remark was deleted; however, the perceptions formed in the minds of many had become inalterable.

A.H. Sayce concludes, in *The Races of the Old Testament,* that with the exceptions of the Nubians all divisions of mankind were of the White race. His book is filled with racist statements of which we will cite a few examples:

> The Nubians, in spite of their black skins, are usually classed among the handsomest of mankind, just as the negroes are among the ugliest.[37]

When Sayce referred to the Nubians as handsome, he was apparently, mindful of Herodotus' description of the Ethiopians (Nubians) as the tallest, most beautiful and long lived of the human races"[38] as well as to Homer's description of them as "the most just of men; the favorite of the gods."[39] Sayce did not classify the Nubians with the Negro or White race but rather to a separate, distinct race. With regard to the ethnicity of the Nubians he commented:

Racially and linguistically they stand apart from the rest of mankind. Just as their languages form an isolated family of speech, so too, on the ethnological, they form a separate race. [40]

Sayce claimed that the so called Ethiopian Dynasty of Egypt really consisted of kings of Cush, "These kings, like the court which surrounded them, belong to the white race."[41] Conversely, elsewhere Sayce stated, 'the Ethiopian' who saved the life of Jeremiah, was probably a negro (Jer. 38:7-13), like Cush "the Cushite," the great grandfather of Jehudi "the Jew" (Jer. 36:14).[42] Sayce taught that Ethiopians were members of the White race, but among the natives of "Cush" [Ethiopia] were black-skinned negroes and Nubians, though the main bulk of the population was of Semitic of Egyptian descent."[43]

Sayce did not attempt to camouflage his belief that Negroes are intellectually inferior to other races. He stated,

He has but little sympathy for art, except music, of which he is passionately fond. He is moved by emotion rather than argument, and it is alleged that Negro children seldom advance in their studies after the age fourteen. In character the Negro is indolent, superstitious, affectionate, and faithful. The two latter qualities have caused him to be sought after as a slave or servant. [44]

In another passage he wrote, "The Negro, indeed, could not have designed, much less achieved, either the rock paintings of the Bushmen, or the rock engravings of Northern Africa."[45] However, Sayce who staunchly believed in the intellectual incapability of the Negro stated: "and yet there have been Negroes like Toussaint or a recent ambassador from Liberia [Dr. E. W. Blyden] who have shown themselves equals in intellectual power of the most cultivated Europeans."[46] We could cite many other racist viewpoints expressed by Sayce. He made a comment that is difficult to digest since he made so many racist remarks. Nevertheless, Sayce was sincere in his beliefs and his Christianity. He was also sincerely wrong in academically denying Blacks a heritage in the biblical world. Sayce quoted Acts 17:26 with a positive comment as he concluded his chapter on "Language and Race."

God "hath made of one blood all nations of men for to dwell on all the face of the earth." Black or white, red, or yellow, we are all bound together by a common nature; we can all alike claim a common ancestry, and recognize that we have each been made 'in the image' of the Creator. [47]

Sayce admitted,

The fact that the races are all divisions of the White races intro-
duces us to one of those defects in ethnological terminology
which show how young the science of ethnology must still be. It
has not as of yet acquired a settled and defined terminology such
as shall be understood alike by the ethnological student and the
ordinary educated reader....in the science of ethnology we want
some term which shall distinguish a race, in the usual acceptation
of the word, from those larger divisions of mankind which stand
to them in the relation of a genus to a species.[48]

Sayces's comments regarding "defects in ethnological terminology" and the difficulty in labeling the different divisions of the "white
races", in our opinion is a subtle admission that the Whites who he has
labeled "White" were really not White, but until another appellation is
designated he would keep labeling all the races of the biblical world White.
To label people who are black, brown, red and even light yellow with kinky
or curly hair "White" is scholastically dishonest, and inconsistent with
"usual acceptation" of race. When White scholars conclude that the
prominent people of the biblical and ancient world were "White" or
"Caucasoid" despite the nontypical Caucasoid features of the people, they
are committing a blatant act of racism almost comparable to the acts of
racism perpetrated on Blacks and other non-Whites, by the Ku Klux Klan.
Although unintentional, those in White academia and who have utilized
Grolier Encyclopedia's broad definition of Caucasian, have in effect served
as the academic and public relations arm of racist organizations. Again, we
recognize that this was certainly not the intent of most of the White
commentators, however such beliefs gave rise to a mindset that Blacks are
inferior.

We have watched biblical movies produced in Hollywood all of
our lives. The characters generally are Euro-American. Rarely are they
Africans, Asians, Arabs, Palestinian, or Jews. Certainly, Europeans were
present in the biblical world, but to leave out other races is an historically
inaccurate and dishonest portrayal of biblical history. This is WRONG!
White academia, "Hollywood" and the church must repent for propagat-
ing a view of history that is inconsistent with Scripture, especially ethno-
logically.

Lest it is thought that we are being unforgiving toward White
academia, Martin Bernal, a White Jewish scholar echoes the same sentiments in his book *Black Anthena Vol.II* published by Rutgers University
Press. Bernal affirmed that Greece was originally inhabited by Pelasgian
and other primitive tribes. "These [indigenous Grecian tribes] had been

civilized by Egyptian and Phonecian settlers who had ruled many parts of the country during the heroic age."[49] Bernal called this viewpoint the "Ancient Model" which simply meant that Egyptian and Phonecian settlers, in "Civilized" Greece were the ones who brought a high culture to the region.[50] The concept of the "Ancient Model" (regarding Greece's origin and development) was the popular belief in Greece from 5th century Greece until the end of the 18th century. However, this belief was over-thrown in the 1840's and replaced by the "Aryan Model".[51]

The "Aryan Model" stated that Greek civilization resulted from cultural mixing following the conquest by Indo-European speaking Greeks from the earlier 'Pre-Hellenic' peoples. To make the distinction between these two models even more vivid, the "Ancient Model" postulates that Greece was civilized by Egyptians and Phonecians (people of color) and the "Aryan Model" maintains that Greece was civilized or developed by Indo-Europeans, the Pre-Hellenic (White) people! Remember the "Aryan Model" was not proposed until the 19th century and "Ancient Model" existed in Greece from the 5th-8th century. Bernal contends that "most of the men who established the Aryan Model were–to put it bluntly–racist and anti-Semites."[52] Bernal boldly calls persons who developed the "Aryan Model", which denies that people of color (Egyptians and Phonecians) settled and developed Greece, racist.

We do not believe that persons who deny or argue against the Black presence in Scripture are racist. Some of the people we quoted, we know personally and have never experienced a hint of racism in our dealings with them. Nevertheless, we believe that if they seriously weigh all the evidence and objectively study the presence of Blacks in the Bible, most of them would arrive at a different conclusion.

The Ancient and Aryan Models postulated by Bernal reminds us of the Old Hamite and New Hamite viewpoints postulated by Dr. Charles B. Copher. Indeed, the parallels are undeniable. Dr. Copher was the second Black man in the country to receive a doctorate in Old Testament from Boston University in 1947. Stated briefly, the Old Hamite view, according to Copher states, "the Hamites referred to in the Bible were people black in color, and generally regarded as what were called Ne-groes."[53] Thus, the Hamites listed in the biblical Table of Nations in-cluded: Egyptians, African Cushites (Ethiopians), and Asiatic Cushites of South Asia, Mesopotamia, Phonecia and Canaan. These are the people regarded as the founders of the great ancient civilizations of the Middle East.[54]

The New Hamite View was introduced around 1800 B.C. accord-ing to Copher and, "dissociates the so-called Negroes from the Hamites, removes color from the criteria for determining racial identity, and regards black, non-Negroids to be white -Caucasoid or Europic Blacks."[55] Just as the Aryan Model replaced the Ancient Model in popular and scholarly thought regarding the study of Greece in modern times, so has been the New Hamite viewpoint which was replaced by the old Hamite viewpoint regarding the presence of Blacks and other people of color in the Bible in popular and scholarly thought. In 1891 A.H. Sayce stated:

> It is but recently that ethnologist have discovered that the Egyptian is a member of the white race. Indeed, professor Virchow has been the first to prove that such is the case....Prof. Virchow has shown the Egyptian, like the Canaanite, belongs to the white race.[56]

In the preface of his first edition Sayce revealed "Ethnology itself is but a young science, still busied in collecting its facts and arranging its materials; Biblical ethnology is younger still. Indeed, it is only within the last three to four years that a study of the ethnology of the Old Testament has become possible."[57] Copher validated the same truth. It was not until the 1800's that ethnologists classified the Egyptians as a member of the white race. It was also during that time that all the Hamites were academically removed from the Negro race and placed with the White race. If it was not until the 1800's that academia decided the Egyptians and the Canaanites were White, what was the name for their race before the 1800's? And if they were White, why did Professor Virchow have to "prove" that such was the case? Would it not have been obvious?

In elaborating upon the "new Hamite hypothesis" or the view which dissociates Negroes from Hamites and removes color from the criteria for determining racial identity, Copher wrote:

> It is this view or hypothesis which came to characterize the so-called science of anthropology, ethnology, and kindred studies, but also critical historical-literary Biblical studies. And just as anthropology and ethnology removed Negroes from the Biblical world so did critical study of the Bible remove Negroes from the Bible and Biblical history except for the occasional Negro individual who could only have been a slave. Thus, today in critical Biblical studies, as in anthropology and ethnology, the ancient Egyptians, Cushites, in fact all the Biblical Hamites, were Whites; so-called Negroes did not figure at all in Biblical history....[58]

It is the new Hamite view that allows Sayce to make obvious contradictory statements which we suppose are academically respected. In contrasting the Nubians and Negroes, Sayce commented:

It will be seen that in their physical characteristics they form a striking contrast to the Negro, the black skin and hair alone excepted.[59]

Although Negroes and Nubians shared "black skin and hair", that was not enough to classify them as the same racially. By removing color as a criteria for racial classifications, the new Hamite theory allowed White academia to classify any group they chose to be White which is why the *Grolier Encyclopedia* list such Negroes as the Australian aborigines, the Berbers, Hamites and Indians as Caucasoid.[60]

It is essential to keep in mind that when White academia formed such inclusive and broad definitions of race in the 1800's and declared (as Sayce and Albright did) that all races of the biblical world were White (with the possible exception of the Cushites or Nubians for some), they were utilizing a textbook definition of race. They developed the theory to suit their purposes and not the working and commonly accepted definitions of race. If the definition of Caucasoid or Caucasians was utilized in America to determine racial classifications as it was by European and Euro-American scholars, the Negro population in America would almost be nonexistent.

We question why was there a shift from the Old Hamite view to the New Hamite view? Who authorized the shift? Were Blacks and other people of color included in the discussions, and if so, did they give consent to the shift? Is their some commonality to the shift from Bernal's Ancient Model to the Aryan Model in the 1800's, and the shift from Copher's Old Hamite view to the New Hamite view in the 1800's? Is it purely coincidental that academia shifted from the "Ancient Model to the Aryan Model" during the same time that the church shifted from the "Old Hamite View" to the "New Hamite View"? Was the shift related to the fact that in spite of the laws forbidding Blacks to read, they inevitably read the Bible? Did the shift take place when it was realized that Blacks in America discovered that they were a part of God's divine plan as they were descendants of Ham? Did the shift take place when it was known that Blacks discovered they were genetically related to the great ancient kingdoms of Ethiopia, Egypt, Canaan, Mesopotamia, Babylon and the Phonecian people? Was critical theology the driving force behind the "shift" or was it the agenda of the White supremacist? Did secular academia influence the church to change her mind regarding the ethnicity of Noah's descendants or did the church influence secular academia? Nevertheless, a shift took place and inherent in that shift was the raping of a culture of its historical biblical roots.

Since color was not the criteria for racial identity in the New Hamite View, the people of dark complexions can be classified as White.

The New Hamite View was certainly the academic justification used by ISBE to classify all Africans in the biblical world as Caucasoid. Even the woman Moses married, the "Cushite" was said to be Caucasoid regardless of the definition for Cushite: a term probably implying a dark skinned Egyptian, descendant of Nubians."[61] If dark complexioned people in North Africa were categorized as Caucasoid, why are the dark complexioned people in America labeled Black and not caucasoid? Persons born in America who are dark skinned with curly hair are never legally classified as Caucasians; therefore, what is the justification or rationale for classifying the people in biblical times, with similar features, as Caucasians? We long for White academia to provide rational and consistent answers to these questions.

According to Martin Bernal, J.F. Blumenbach, a professor of natural history at Gottingen was the first to publicize the term 'Caucasian', in 1795. [62] According to Blumenbach, "the White or Caucasian was the first and most beautiful and talented race, from which all the others had degenerated to become, Chinese, Negroes, etc."[63] Men like Blumenbach make it absolutely necessary for Blacks to define themselves, in order to preserve biblical accuracy.

The Dakes Annotated Reference Bible (DARB), examined Genesis 9:18-27 and made the following annotation:

All colors and types of men came into existence after the flood. All men were white up to this point, for there was only one family line - that of Noah who was White and in the line of Christ, being mentioned in Luke 3:36 with his son Shem....[There is a] prophecy that Shem would be a chosen race and have a peculiar relationship with God [v.26]. All divine revelation since Shem has come through this line....[There is a] prophecy that Japheth would be the father of the great and enlarged races [v.27]. Government, Science and Art are mainly Japhetic....His descendants constitute the leading nations of civilization.[64]

Blumenbach and DARB agree that Whites were the first persons on earth and the leading race of civilization. DARB maintains that Noah was White and therefore the line of Christ. John MacArthur has gone through personal suffering for his public stance with Black Christian leaders against the sin of racism. Yet he is viewed by some as reinforcing the notion that Jesus was White in his book *God With Us*:

Here's a side to the Christmas story that isn't often told: Those soft little hands, fashioned by the Holy Spirit in Mary's womb, were made so that nails might be driven through them. Those baby feet, pink and unable to walk, would one day walk up a dusty hill to be nailed to a cross. [65]

The question is raised as to what foundation did John MacArthur base his claim that Jesus' feet were "pink"? This is certainly not how the Apostle John described the feet of the glorified Jesus (Rev. 1:15). We realize that MacArthur was reflecting the New Hamite View of the White cultural milieu, rather than just an academic statement. Nevertheless, this underscores why White evangelicals need to become increasingly mindful of the diversity of their audiences. There should be a sensitivity to those who cannot identify with feet that are "pink," skin that is "white," or hair that is "straight" particularly when there is strong evidence to the contrary. This is especially true since many Black Muslims have harangued to Blacks that it is psychologically unhealthy to worship and serve a blond haired, blue-eyed, "pink" Jesus, for it is tantamount to serving slave oppressors.

Today, if there are Whites who may be critical of this viewpoint, they should first examine the reverse viewpoint, the worship of a brown-skinned, wooly-haired Jesus by White biblical scholars. If Jesus were depicted in this manner it would probably be a hinderance to White evangelism.

John Walvoord in his book *The Nations, Israel and the Church in Prophecy* wrote "The sons of Japheth were more prolific in number than any of the other sons of Noah..." [66] We do not believe that Walvoord attempted to falsely enhance the descendants of Japheth. To have suggested that the Japhetites were more prolific in number than the sons of Ham is an innocent mistake on Walvoord's part. Japheth's descendants do not outnumber Shem's or Ham's descendants in Scripture or in the modern world. Our concern is that the uncritical reader will accept Walvoord's statement and will be misled as to the significance of the population in the biblical and modern world.

J. Vernon McGee, a fellow Dallas Seminary alumnus, expressed an opposing viewpoint from Walvoord's concerning the descendants of the sons of Noah based on the Table of Nations in Genesis chapter ten:

In chapter 10, seventy nations are listed. Fourteen of them are from Japheth. Thirty of them come from Ham. Don't forget that. It will give you a different conception of the black man at his beginning. And twenty-six nations come from Shem, making a total of seventy nations listed in this genealogy. ...It seems to me that God is showing us what He has done with the nations of the world. Why has the White man in our day been so prominent? Well, I'll tell you why. Because at the beginning it was the Black man, the colored races that were prominent....Apparently we are currently in the period in which the White man has come to the front. It seems to me that all three are demonstrating that, regardless of whether they are a son of Ham, or a son of Shem, or a son of Japheth, they are incapable of ruling this world. I believe that God is demonstrating this to us, and to see this, is a tremendous thing.[67]

If one accepts the Old Hamite view, politically, numerically, and culturally, they will deduce that the people of dark complexions were the dominant people of the ancient world and the fathers of civilized society as we know it today.

The World Book Encyclopedia states that the Hamites refer to race only as opposed to language only. [68] Merit Students Encyclopedia informs us that Hamites refer to language only.[69] Encyclopedia Americana records:

Hamites - the name given to several non-Negroid ethnic groups in northern and eastern Africa who are regarded to be of kindred origin and who speak allied languages.[70]

Collier's Encyclopedias reports that "Ham was the progenitor of one of the three great races of the world, the inhabitants of the African continent."[71] The Encyclopedia Americana limits Hamites to northern and eastern Africa. Collier maintains that Hamites were dispensed throughout the African continent--which would inevitably include black people. Again, the encyclopedia's do not speak with a consistent voice regarding the "Hamites".

The above four encyclopedic references document the fact that if one depends solely upon scholarly opinions to draw final conclusions regarding Ham and the Hamites, confusion will ensue. This confusion concerning the Hamites originates with academia itself. The original disagreement came about by the shifting from the Old Hamite View to the New Hamite View, without sound research and reasoning. The New Hamite view has become the predominant viewpoint believed and taught on most Christian college campuses today, including Southwestern Seminary in Fort Worth. Students who take the Biblical Background class are required to read The MacMillan Bible Atlas by Yohanan Aharoni and Miachel Avi-Yonah (both professors of archaeology in universities in Israel at the time of publication). In the Atlas, there are three relics pictured representing "Japheth - Cretan", "Ham - Ti", and "Shem - Assyrian". These pictures obviously reflect a White European, a Black African, and a dusky olive Middle-Eastern. It is clear that all three relics of races cannot be classified Caucasian. Inconsistent, illogical, and insensitive conclusions abound in White academia particularly regarding Ham and his descendants. Unfortunately thousands of students emerge from these schools confused or either virtually ignorant regarding biblical ethnicity.

People of color in Scripture are stripped of any possibility of being from the line of Ham or Black. This is usually the method used by many commentators to cast doubt upon the minds of their students. *The Bible Knowledge Commentary* with regard to Numbers chapter twelve--the complexion of the Cushite wife:

> The Cushites were not necessarily a different color since people of that name existed in early times in Arabia as well as Cush proper (what is today southern Egypt, Sudan and northern Ethiopia). [73]

Why did this commentary find it necessary to clarify that the Cushites were not necessarily a different color from Moses? Did the commentators feel it would be wrong or embarrassing to reveal Moses and his bride were from different races? Does the probability that Moses' bride, the Cushite, being a native of Arabia or Asiatic Cush means that her color was identical to Moses' or her color automatically became lighter? *Dakes Bible* specifically states this woman "was not of the Negro race."[74] R.K. Harrison stated in *The Wycliffe Exegetical Commentary*, Numbers:

> If the woman whom Moses had married was indeed a descendant of Cush, she could trace her line back to Ham, a son of Noah (Gen. 10:1). The Hamites lived principally in Nubia or Ethiopia.... the scornful appellation 'Cushite' might suggest racial discrimination on the part of Miriam, but if the woman came from ancient Ethiopia or Nubia her physiognomy would be little different from that of Miriam herself, since the people living on the southern border of Egypt were not distinctively Negroid....If the color of skin and shape of facial features was a factor, the term 'Cushite' could also have been applied equally well to the Midianites, who were tanned nomads from northwest Arabia.[75]

Apparently, Harrison adheres to the New Hamite View which removes color as a criteria for racial classifications (at least in the biblical world) because he concedes that the woman could have been a descendant of Ham, Nubia, Ethiopia or "tanned" and yet not be "distinctively Negroid." How could "Cushite" be a "scornful appellation" when the Cushites were of high standing according to the Table of Nations in Genesis 10:6-12? When Harrison claimed that the woman came from

Ethiopia or Nubia and her physiognomy would be little different from Miriam's (and in effect Moses), is he saying that Miriam and Moses looked like Ethiopians? And if Moses, Miriam, and the "Cushite" lady were all similar in color as Harrison and *The Bible Knowledge Commentary* suggest, then what color were they? And if the color of a typical Nubian or Ethiopian was "tanned", then Moses, his wife, and Miriam, for that matter, could have met the popular definition for "Negro" today. Thank God, for men like Martin Bernal who emphatically stated in a discussion regarding the ethnicity of the Cushites, Nubian, Ethiopians, Midianites and the Kassites:

> ...the darker Midianites to the southeast of Canaan, many of whom, like the South Arabians of today, resembled Somalis and other Northeast Africans. [76]

At the time of this writing, American troops are positioned in Somalia; and it is clear to television viewers the features and race of the Somalis. If Bernal is correct in his view that the Cushites and Midianites resembled the Somalis of our time, we see a stark conflict with the views of *Dakes'*, *The Bible Knowledge Commentary* and Harrison. We also see the effort placed by *Dakes'*, *The Bible Knowledge Commentary* and Harrison on the view that the Cushite woman was not black. If Bernal could compare the resemblance of South Arabians of today to the Somalis, why could not *The Bible Knowledge Commentary*? To use the view that the Cushite woman descended from South Arabia is a subtle indication that she could not have possibly been Negro. We have studied modern and ancient ethnicity enough to know that it is not uncommon for many southern Arabians to be identical to their East African counterparts and both reflect distinct Negroid features. Most Black Americans would be alarmed to discover that the majority of western academia would not consider the Somalis and other Northeast African people, who look just like them, as Black or Negroid.

Before we move on we must comment on the implications growing out of Harrison's comments as well as from *The Bible Knowledge Commentary*. The implication is that Moses and Miriam (Jews-Semites) were perhaps similar in color to the Cushites, Midianites, and the Somalis (Hamites). We must reference Bernal again to testify about a Negro admixture in the bloodline of the biblical Israelites. He wrote:

> The name Pinhas [Phinehas] also cast an interesting light on the 'racial' make-up of this population [Exodus population] with its indication that there were people with pigmentation darker than

the Mediterranean norm, but that this feature was uncommon enough to be remarkable.[77]

The name Phinehas means "the Nubian" or "the Negro" according to the ISBE. [78] Bernal stated the first use of this name was for the grandson of Aaron referred to in Exodus. [79] William F. Albright wrote: "The name Phineas...is interesting as providing an independent (and absolutely reliable) confirmation of the tradition that there was a Nubian element in the family of Moses (Num.12:1). [80] As a matter of fact Moses himself testifies concerning the ethnicity of the people who departed Egypt on the Exodus journey to Canaan land; "And a mixed multitude went up also with them." (Ex. 12:38). This "mixed multitude" would include native born Egyptians from the land of Ham and descendants of 400 years of miscegenation between the Egyptians and Israelites.

Therefore, if Moses and Miriam resembled the Cushites and Somalis, it is because the Israelites and Egyptians ascended from Egypt a "mixed multitude". Even A.H. Sayce argues, "The thickness or fullness of the lips again is a racial feature, characteristic of the African, and found also in the Egyptian and Jew."[81] We believe the dominant Jewish complexion was "dusky or olive colored", a little lighter than the average Negro. But, where there was significant and long term mixing of the races, the Israelite population darkened and eventually formed racial features similar to the Midianites, Cushites and Somalis. Many of the Somalis do not have strongly pronounced Negroid features, but that is also true of many Black Americans and Africans. And of course, there is a remote chance that when *The Bible Knowledge Commentary* suggested that Moses and his Cushite wife were not necessarily a different color, they may have been suggesting Moses and his Cushite wife were both White. [82]

In his introduction to the book of Zephaniah, Harrison commented:

> There appears to be little ground for the supposition of Bentzen, that Cushi, his father, was actually an Ethiopian; and that Zephaniah was a Negro slave in the service of the Temple. [83]

With these thirty two words, Harrison dismisses any possibility that the prophet Zephaniah was a Negro. He offers no other thought on the probable Black ancestry of the prophet Zephaniah. On the contrary the White, Old Testament Professor, Dr. Gene Rice wrote a thorough investigation into *The African Roots of the Prophet Zephaniah*, and concluded:

> The roots of the prophet Zephaniah is not the only subject of the Bible that does not permit the satisfaction of a definitive answer.

A careful examination of this matter, however, points persuasively to the conclusion that he was of both royal and Ethiopian ancestry. [84]

According to Frank Snowden, John Chrysostom pointed to the eunuch [Acts 8:26-39] as one who, "though a barbarian without advantages, read the Scriptures in spite of other important matters occupying his attention."[85]   "Barbarian"? The eunuch was reading from a Greek Bible (Septuagint), in a chauffeur driven chariot, and he was leaving Jerusalem after worshipping the God of Abraham, Isaac and Jacob. "Barbarian"?

Finally, Harry Ironside, in his commentary on Acts, created a dialogue between Phillip and the eunuch. Phillip asked the eunuch, "Do you understand what you are reading?" The Ethiopian looked at him, doubtless in amazement, saying, "How can I, except some man should guide me? I AM A POOR IGNORANT MAN FROM ETHIOPIA. Oh, that I had someone to explain the words to me!" [86]

Ironside put words in this man's mouth and made him claim that he was "poor and ignorant." Poor he was not for he served his country as the Chief Minister of Finance. Ignorant he was not. It is believed that he returned to the regions of Ethiopia and there he founded the Coptic Church. A National Geographic television documentary Fact Sheet stated:

Christianity took root in Ethiopia, 1,400 years before missionaries first arrived in Africa. [87]

This man as a descendant of Ham fulfilled the Davidic prophecy that "Princes shall come out of Egypt and the Ethiopian shall soon stretch out his hand to God" (Psalm 68:31). Unfortunately, Blacks who rely upon popular commentaries from Aryan Models and the New Hamite View are denied the right to claim the Ethiopian eunuch as a biblical ancestor.

Finally, men of integrity and sound scholarship can no longer support such outrageous fallacies seen in the Aryan Model as well as in the New Hamite View. We must proclaim unashamedly our ancestral inclusion into the lineage of Christ and our presence in Holy Scripture. We owe these truths to our children so that they will not be deprived of their heritage.

1. Stan Harris, "How Shall I Curse the Blacks Whom God Hath Not?" Sermon on Cassette, April 1990.

2. Bernard Cousins of Dallas, Texas, shared this information with me during a personal conversation in Dallas in February 1992.

3. "Africa," The International Standary Bible Encyclopedia, William B. Eerdmans Publishing Company, Grand Rapids, MI, rev. 1979, Vol. 1, p. 63.

4. Ibid., p. 63.

5. "Caucasoid," Grolier Universal Encyclopedia, American Book-Stratford Press, Inc., New York, 1966, Vol. 2, p. 518.

6. "Black 'White' Man Challenges Federal Race Identity Law," Jet Magazine, January 7, 1991, p. 8.

7. Ibid., p. 8.

8. A New Standard Bible Dictionary in a section called "Ethnography and Ethnology" and a subsection called "The White, Yellow, and Black Races," says, "...in very remote times, there arose three well differentiated human strains, corresponding to the three great continental areas: a white race in Europe, a yellow race in Asia, and a black race in Africa. Within historical times, however, these strains have always been blended in an infinite variety of combinations. By Europe, we mean EuraAfrica, or Europe plus the northwest corner of Africa..." Funk & Wagnalls Co., New York and London, 1930, p. 233.

9. The International Standard Bible Encyclopedia, Vol. 1, p. 63.

10. Ibid., p. 65.

11. "Ham", Pictorial Bible Dictionary, The Southwestern Company, Nashville, TN, 1975, p. 330.

12. T. Alton Bryant (ed.), "Ham", The New Compact Bible Dictionary, Zondervan Publishing House, Grand Rapids, MI, 1987, p. 213.

13. The Living Bible, Tyndale House Publishers, Wheaton, IL, 1971, p. 7.

14. "Hamite", Webster's Students Dictionary, American Book Company, 1959, p. 370.

15. T.B. Maston, The Bible and Race, Broadman Press, Nashville, TN, 1959, p. 114.

16. Raymond H. Woolsey, "Men and Women of Color in the Bible," International Bible, Inc., Langley Park, MD, 1977, Special Section, p. 13, cited in The Holy Bible, Authorized King James Version, Heritage Edition, Stampley Enterprises, Inc., Charlotte, NC, 1977.

17. "Ham", The International Standard Bible Encyclopedia, Vol. 2, p. 601.

18. Clem Davies, The Racial Streams of Mankind, Graphic Press, Los Angeles, CA, 1946, pp. 1, 6, 7, 11.

19. Ibid., p. 6.

20. Ibid., pp. 18-19.

21. Ibid., p. 21.

22. Ibid., p. 21.

23. Ibid., p. 6.

24. Aubrey de Selincourt, Herodotus the Histories, Penguin Books, Harmondsworth, Middlesex, England, 1972, p. 167.

25. C. F. Keil & F. Delitzsch, Commentary on the Old Testament, Vol. 1, The Pentateuch, Translated by James Martin, Hendrickson Publishers, Peabody, MA, 1989, pp. 157-158.

26. Ibid., p. 164.

27. I. Epstein, ed., Hebrew-English Edition of the Babylonian Talmud, trans. Jacob Shacter and H. Freedman, rev. ed. (London: The Soncino Press, 1969), Sanhedrin 108b. The explanatory footnote states, "i.e., from him descended Cush (the negro) who is black-skinned." quoted by Charles B. Copher, Stony the Road We Trod - African Amerian Biblical Interpretation, Fortress Press, Minneapolis, MN, 1991, p. 147, ed. by C.H. Felder.

28. Peterson (Look at 41, p. 431)

29. Gene Rice, "The Curse That Never Was," The Journal of Religious Thought, Vol. 50, 1972, p. 17.

30. Thomas Virgil Peterson, Ham and Japheth: The Mythic World of Whites in the Antebellum South, ATLA Monograph Series, No. 12, The Scarecrow Press, Inc. and The American Theological Library Assoc., Metuchen, NJ & London, 1978, pp. 43, 44, 73.

31. Ibid., pp. 44, 74.

32. Ed. by C. I. Scofield, The Scofield Reference Bible: The Holy Bible, Oxford University Press, New York, 1945, p. 16.

33. Arthur W. Pink, Gleanings in Genesis, Moody Press, Chicago, 1981, p. 125.

34. Robert Jamieson, A.R. Fausset, David Brown, Commentary on the Whole Bible, Regency Reference Library, Zondervan Publishing House, Grand Rapids, MI, 1961, p. 24.

35. C. I. Scofield, The Scofield Reference Bible, (New York: Oxford University Press, 1917), 16.

36. Ernest R. Sandeen, The Roots of Fundamentalism, (Chicago: University of Chicago Press, 1970), 222.

37. Ibid., p. 81.

38. Jackson, p. 65.

39. Ibid.

40. Sayce, p. 210.

41. Ibid., p. 209.

42. Ibid., p. 212.

43. Ibid., pp. 70, 81.

44. Ibid., p. 211.

45. Ibid., p. 215.

46. Ibid., p. 42.

47. Ibid., pp. 61-63.

48. Ibid., p. 238.

49. Martin Bernal, Black Athena: The Afroasiatic Roots of Classical Civilization, Vol. 1, The Fabrication of Ancient Greece 1785-1985, Rutgers University Press, New Brunswick, NJ, 1987, p. 1.

50. Martin Bernal, Black Athena: The Afroasiatic Roots of Classical Civilization, Vol. II, The Archaeological and Documentary Evidence, Rutgers University Press, New Brunswick, NJ, 1991, p.1.

51. Ibid.

52. Ibid., p. 2.

53. Charles B. Copher, Black Biblical Studies: An Anthology of Charles B. Copher, Biblical and Theological Issues on the Black Presence in the Bible, Black Light Fellowship, Chicago, IL, 1993, p. 34.

54. Ibid., pp. 34-35.

55. Ibid., p. 35.

56. Sayce, pp. 68, 127.

57. Sayce, Preface iii.

58. Copher, Black Biblical Studies, p. 35.

59. Sayce, p. 82.

60. "Caucasoid", Grolier Universal Encyclopedia, 1966, Vol. 2, p. 518.

61. "Africa", The International Standard Bible Encyclopedia, Vol. 1, p. 65.

62. Martin Bernal, Black Athena: The Afroasiatic Roots of Classical Civilization, Vol. 1, The Fabrication of Ancient Greece 1785-1985, Rutgers University Press, New Brunswick, NJ, 1987, p. 219.

63. Ibid.

64. Finis Jennings Dake, Dake's Annotated Reference Bible, Dake Bible Sales, Inc., Lawrenceville, GA, 1981, pp. 8, 9, 36,40 quoted by Cain Hope Felder, p. 132.

65. John F. MacArthur, Jr., God With Us: The Miracle of Christmas, Zondervan Publishing House, Grand Rapids, MI, 1989, p. 116.

66. John F. Walvoord, The Nations, Israel and the Church in Prophecy, Academic Books, Zondervan Publishing House, Grand Rapids, MI, 1967, p. 26.

67. J. Vernon McGee, Thru the Bible with J. Vernon McGee, Vol. 1, Genesis-Deuteronomy, Thomas Nelson Publishers, Nashville, 1981, pp. 51-52.

68. "Hamites", The World Book Encyclopedia, 1990, Vol. 9, p. 33.

69. "Hamites", Merit Students Encyclopedia, MacMillan Educational Co., 1987, Vol. 8, p. 378.

70. "Hamitic Peoples", Encyclopedia Americana, Grolier Inc., 1992, Vol. 13, p. 742.

71. "Ham", Collier's Encyclopedia, MacMillan Educational Co., 1991, vol. 11, p. 603.

72. Yohanan Aharoni & Michael Avi-Yonah, The MacMillan Bible Atlas, Revised Edition, MacMillan Publishing Co., Inc., New York, 1968, p. 15.

73. John F. Walvoord & Roy B. Zuck, The Bible Knowledge Commentary: An Exposition of the Scriptures by Dallas Seminary Faculty, Old Testament, Victor Books, SP Publications, Inc., Wheaton, IL, 1986, 3rd Printing, 1986, p. 228.

74. Finis Jennings Dake, Dake's Annotated Reference Bible, p. 169, quoted by David Tuesday Adamo, p. 121.

75. R.K. Harrison, The Wycliffe Exegetical Commentary, Numbers, ed. by Kenneth Barker, Moody Press, Chicago, 1990, p. 195.

76. Bernal, Vol. II, p. 253.

77. Bernal, Vol. II, p. 333.

78. "Phinehas", International Standard Bible Encyclopedia, 1986, Vol. 3, p. 94.

79. Bernal, Vol. II, p. 333.

80. William Foxwell Albright, From the Stone Age to Christianity: Monotheism and the Historical Process, The John Hopkins Press, Baltimore, 1946, 193f, idem, Yahweh and the Gods of Canaan: A Historical Analysis of Two Contrasting Faiths, Doubleday and Company, Inc., Garden City, N.Y., 1968, p. 165, quoted by Charles B. Copher, p. 155.

81. Sayce, p. 33.

82. John F. Walvoord and Roy B. Zuck (ed.), The Bible Knowledge Commentary: An Exposition of the Scriptures by Dallas Seminary Faculty, Old Testament, Victor Books, Wheaton, IL, 1986, p. 228.

83. R. K. Harrison, Introduction to the Old Testament, William B. Eerdmans Publishing Company, Grand Rapids, MI, 1969, p. 234.

84. Gene Rice, "The African Roots of the Prophet Zephaniah," The Journal of Religious Thought, 36, No. 1 (Spring-Summer 1979), pp. 21-31.

85. Frank M. Snowden, Jr., Before Color Prejudice: The Ancient View of Blacks, Harvard University Press, Cambridge, MA, 1983, p. 105.

86. H. A. Ironside, Lectures on the Book of Acts, Loizeaux Brothers, New Jersey, 1988, p. 194.

87. N.H. Cominos, "Ethiopia: The Hidden Empire," National Geographic Society Documentary Special, Metromedia Producers Corporation.

Chapter 3

A GLIMMER OF HOPE

It is necessary to uncover and evaluate the seldom taught view-points of European and Euro-American scholars regarding ancient ethnicity, especially the subject of Blacks in the Bible. Furthermore, it is our intention to challenge the White Christian community to inform their constituencies of biblical ethnicity in order to affirmatively impact modern day race relations.

The Emancipation and Civil Rights movements in America were greatly aided by objective, progressive and fair-minded Whites. Similarly, the discussion of Blacks in the Bible and the ancient world has also been greatly aided by objective White scholars. The Bible, rightly interpreted, unfolds gloriously a historical contribution of the Black race to the biblical world. On the other hand, conversely, the Bible wrongly interpreted, denies the biblical heritage of the Black race while giving Europeans and other races an origin and identity of which they can be proud. Certainly, we are not attempting to deny or denigrate the positive and significant contributions of Anglos to the biblical world, but neither can we be silent as to the positive and significant contributions of Africans.

Jesus said, "And ye shall know the truth, and the truth shall make you free" (John 8:32). Only knowing the truth will set us free. It is our goal in this chapter to share positive truths about the identity and contributions of Blacks in the ancient days of Bible history, in order to set people free from unbiblical, illogical and historically inaccurate thinking.

We owe a great debt of gratitude to the late J. Vernon McGhee for having the courage to confront this subject. In his commentary on the book of Genesis, McGhee succinctly confirmed our convictions:

> The first great civilization, therefore, came out from the sons of Ham. We need to recognize that. It is so easy today to fall into the old patterns that we were taught in school a few years ago. Now the black man is wanting more study of his race. I don't blame him. He hasn't been given an opportunity in the past several hundred years. The story of the beginning of the black man is that he headed up the first two great civilizations that appeared on this earth. They were from the sons of Ham. Nimrod was a son of Ham. I'm not going to attempt to develop that line any further.[1]

J. Vernon McGhee was a graduate of Dallas Theological Seminary. He was widely respected as a pastor, teacher, lecturer and author. McGhee implicitly admitted that historically an inaccurate view of race has been taught in the American school system. One is left to wonder what might have been the impact on race relations in America if McGhee's view of race had been taught from day one. ...The first two great civilizations headed by the Black man that McGhee refers to are Sumer (Mesopotamia) and Egypt.

Arthur C. Custance, a Canadian, studied toward a Ph.D. in Anthropology from the University of Toronto. His Ph.D. studies were interrupted just prior to the presentation of his thesis by a move to Ottawa. Subsequently, the degree was granted by the University of Ottawa in Education. Custance shares with McGhee his belief that people of color were the originators of civilization:

> The Hamites, according to my thesis, include virtually all the people who in ancient times were the originators and creators of civilization in both the old and the new world. It is this fact, for which we now have massive evidence that comes as such a surprise to most Indo-European readers, and which, in the words of one high Canadian Government authority, came almost as a 'revelation.' Out of Ham have been derived all the so called colored races--'the yellow,' 'red,' 'brown,' and 'black'--the Mongoloid and the Negroid. Their contribution to human civilization in so far as it has to do with technology has been absolutely unsurpassed...The Canaanites and the Sumerians (both descendants of Ham) refer to themselves as 'black headed' people--a designation which seems more likely to have reference to skin color rather than color of hair, since almost all people in this area have black hair anyway; a hair-color distinction would be meaningless... The evidence which does exist, for all its plaucity at times, strongly supports a cradle of mankind in the Middle East from which there went out successive waves of pioneers who were neither Indo-Europeans nor Shemites. These were Hamitic pioneers, either Mongoloid or Negroid in type with some admixture, who blazed trails, and opened up territories in every habitable part of the earth and ultimately established a way of life in each locality which at a basic level made maximum use of the raw materials and resources of that locality... The black people have a quite remarkable series of high cultures to their credit, and are almost born metallurgists... Almost every African community of any size has its own smelting furnace and smithy. No part of this iron working art has been borrowed from Europe. [2]

The study of Scripture (in its original languages) was Arthur C. Custance's most absorbing interest throughout his life. The Canadian government was so impressed with Custance's Ph.D. thesis ("Does Science Transcend Culture?", 1958, which develops the ethnicity and contributions of Noah's sons descendants to civilization) they published for internal use a 250 page report on the matter and supplied it to government research laboratories. We consider Custance's study the singular and most significant writing in existence from the viewpoint of a White evangelical scholar which objectively and comprehensively addresses the contributions of the Hamitic (Black) people in Scripture and ancient history.

C.F. Keil and F. Delitzsch, German old testament scholars, recognized that persons of African descent were not restricted to the continent of Africa during the biblical period. They noted:

> Cush: The Ethiopians of the ancients, who not only dwelt in Africa, but were scattered over the whole of Southern Asia, and originally, in all probability settled in Arabia, where the tribes that still remained, mingled with Shemites, and adopted a Shemitic language. [3]

Many European/Euro-American scholars will acknowledge that the Egyptians called themselves Kemi or Hamites meaning "black." However, they usually assert that the term "black", for the Egyptian, referenced the black soil. In our opinion this is almost always stated in order to erase or barricade from the readers mind any possibility that the skin of the ancient Egyptians were black. However, Keil and Delitzsch recognized a relationship between the Egyptians describing themselves as Kemi (black) to their complexion. They clearly defined the distinction.

> The old Egyptian name is Kemi (Copt, Chemi, Keme), which, Plutarch says, is derived from the dark ash-grey color of the soil covered by the slime of the Nile, but which it is much more correct to trace to Ham, and to regard as indicative of the Hamitic descent of its first inhabitants. [4]

Much of the discussion and often debate regarding Blacks in the Bible centers around Noah's son, Ham. Definitions and opinions rendered regarding Ham's ethnicity and etymology are often contradictory, inconsistent and negative, particularly as it is contrasted with Shem and Japheth (Noah's sons). Colliers Encyclopedia's, in comparison, is revealing and affirmative when pointing to Ham's relationship to the Black race.

...Ham was the progenitor of one of the three great races of the world, the inhabitants of the African continent. The etymology of the name Ham has been the subject of considerable discussion. In the Bible, the phrase 'land of Ham' refers to Egypt (Ps. 105:23; 106:22); and since the Egyptian name for Egypt (Khem, Kem, Chemi, or a variant) is similar, it is thought by many that Ham is its Hebrew form. On this hypothesis, the literal meaning of Ham, like that of Khem, would be 'black.' The reference in Khem, however, is presumably to the blackness of the soil in the Delta region rather than to the darkness of the skin of the inhabitants of Africa; and if Ham is its Hebrew equivalent, it follows that it should be similarly interpreted. [5]

Collier acknowledges that the etymology of Ham has been the subject of much discussion. The definition and history of a race of people pivots on how Ham is historically defined. It is interesting that the ambiguity, controversy, identity, and etymological uncertainty does not exist relative to Noah's sons Japheth and Shem and their descendants or at least not nearly to the same extent. However, only in the references to Ham and the Hamites do we find that most biblical reference sources are negative, illogical and inconsistent.

Among the first Europeans to reflect upon the race of ancient Egyptians in the modern era was Count Constantine de Volney (1757-1820). Volney visited Egypt between 1783 and 1785. He wrote of the brown-skinned Christian Copts, who formed a great part of the non-urban population, that "all have a bloated face, puffed up eyes, flat nose, thick lips; in a word, the true face of the mulatto."[6] The Count was surprised and puzzled at finding in Egypt mulattoes with whom he was familiar only in Europe where such offsprings were a mixture of Caucasian, African or Caribbean blacks. After viewing the Sphinx, he was convinced that a similar process of miscegenation had been at work in Africa, but with Blacks as the majority and Whites the minority in the initial mixture. This led him to write the following words concerning the Sphinx:

> On seeing that head, typically Negro in all its features, I remembered the remarkable passage [of Herodotus]...The ancient Egyptians were true Negroes of the same type as all native born Africans. That being so, we can see how their blood mixed for several centuries with that of the Roman and Greeks, must have lost the intensity of its original color, while retaining nonetheless the imprint of its original mold...What a subject for meditation, to see the present barbarism and ignorance of the Copts, descendants of the alliance between the profound genius of the Egyptians and the brilliant mind of the Greeks! Just think that this race of black

men, today our slave and the object of scorn, is the very race to which we owe our arts, sciences, and even the use of speech! Just imagine, finally, that in the midst of people who call themselves the greatest friends of liberty and humanity that one has approved the most barbarous slavery and questioned whether Black men have the same kind of intelligence as Whites! [7]

Volney cited Herodotus' account of the description of the Egyptians who visited Egypt around 500 B.C.. Herodotus reported that the Colchians and the Egyptians were ethnically the same people based on physical features, cultural practices and language.

My own idea on the subject was based first on the fact that they have black skin and wooly hair...and secondly, and more especially, on the fact that the Colchians, the Egyptians, and the Ethiopians are the only races which from ancient times have practiced circumcision...A further point of resemblance between the Colchians and Egyptians: they share a method of weaving linen different from that of any other people; and there is also similarity between them in language. [8]

Herodotus was an eyewitness to the biblical and ancient world and he had no hesitation to label the Egyptians with "black skins and wooly hair." We find it difficult to understand that with such resources at hand, why should modern scholars fail to make the same acknowledgements?

John Skinner, who in 1910 served as Principal and Professor of Old Testament Language and Literature, Westminster College, Cambridge, made an enlightening comment regarding Kush (Cush) in the Table of Nations (Genesis 10).

There is no reason to doubt that in this verse [Gen. 10:6] the African Kush is meant. That the 'sons' of Kush include Arabian peoples is quite naturally explained by the assumption that the writer believed these Arabs to be of African descent. As a matter of fact, intercourse, involving intermixture of blood, has at all times been common between the two shores of the Red Sea; and indeed the opinion that Africa was the cradle of the Semites has still a measure of scientific support. [9]

In his book *The Races of the Old Testament*, A.H. Sayce's regard for blacks was uncomplimentary and racist. However, he did make a few comments which support positions that we have taken in this book.

The members of the white European race are apt to consider themselves the intellectual leaders of mankind; nevertheless their appearance on the scene of history was relatively late, and the elements of their civilization were derived from the natives of the East... Three thousand years ago a Babylonian or Egyptian traveller in Europe would have had as much reason for assuming the intellectual inferiority of the populations he found there as a modern European traveller has today in the wilds of Southern America. [10]

Sayce also wrote that, "diversity of race must be older than diversity of language"[11] underscoring the fact that racial origins did not begin at or after the Tower of Babel (Gen. 11). According to Sayce, language belonged to the second stage of man's existence when he had become what Aristotle called a "social animal." [12]

H.G. Wells in his book, *A Short History of the World*, stated:

Three main regions and three main kinds of wandering and imperfectly settled people there were in those remote days of the first civilizations in Sumeria and early Egypt. Away in the forest of Europe were the blonde Nordic peoples, hunters and herdsman, a lowly race. This primitive civilization saw very little of this race before 1500 B.C. [13]

Dr. John F. Walvoord, Chancellor of Dallas Theological Seminary, who is considered by theological scholars a leader of conservative theological intelligentsia, taught that "world history since the birth of Christ has largely featured those who were descendants of the seven sons of Japheth."[14] Inherent in his teaching is that prior to the birth of Christ, history featured either the sons of Shem or the sons of Ham, or both. Walvoord further reveals that the sons of Ham inhabited all of Asia (except the north), as well as Southern Europe and Northern Africa. [15]

Unlike many liberal scholars, Walvoord believes Genesis 10 addresses ethnicity and race, not just politics and geography. He confirms:

The record of Genesis 10 is more than an ethnography, that is a description of origin of races, but it is a profound introduction to ethnology, having to do also with the distribution, relationship, and significance of the descendants of Noah in history. [16]

According to Walvoord, the reason Ham's descendants are mostly discussed in Genesis 10 was due to their ultimate relationship to the subsequent history of Israel and the purposes of God in the Middle East. He credits the Hamites as the possible forefathers of the Indians and the racial origin of the "non-Semitic" Ethiopians even though they eventually spoke a Semitic language.[17] He describes Nimrod as a descendant of Cush, originator of Babylon, Mesopotamia, Asshur and Ninevah. He further describes Nimrod as "unquestionably the Napoleon of his day and the head of one of the earliest empires subsequent to Noah recorded in Scripture. His government seems to have occupied most of western Asia and has left many monuments." [18]

Most commentaries are extremely negative toward Nimrod, pointing out all of his faults (and indeed he had some); but Walvoord gives Nimrod the most positive profile by a White scholar to date. True to the text (Gen. 10:8-12, 11:1-9), however, he concludes his discussion of Nimrod stating, "The political might symbolized in Nimrod and his empire was ended subsequent to the divine judgment at the tower of Babel when their one language was confounded." [19] Walvoord links Ham's descendants with prophecy stating the descendants of Put were Africans and God will send them a sign at the beginning of the millennial Kingdom (Is. 66:19, "Phut" spelled "Pul"). "The references to Ethiopia recognize their continued significance in God's program and their ultimate destiny as one of the Gentile nations which will be subordinate to Israel when Christ reigns on earth."[20] In dispensational theology, all nations will be subject to Israel when Christ returns. Walvoord does not specifically state that the Hamites were Black, nor does he state the ethnicity or complexion of the Japhethites or Semites. He does state that Genesis 10 is a description of the origin and distribution of races (p.25).

Religious broadcaster, New York Theological Seminary and Yale Law School graduate, Pat Robertson, who hosts the 700 Club television program leaves no doubt about what he believes about the origin and identity of the races of mankind. In response to the question "Where did all the races come from?" Robertson answers:

> ...Ham became the father of the Egyptians, the Ethiopians, and the other black races, as well as the Canaanites who once lived in the land now occupied by Israel. Japheth was the father of the Greeks, the people who lived in the islands of the sea and who settled Europe and Russia; Shem was the father of the Semitic people-- the Jews, Arabs and Persians. [21]

Keith Irvine, author of, *The Rise of the Colored Races*, was the first White pupil to attend Achimota College in Ghana. [22] He completed his education in Britain, studying at Edinburgh University and later at the Sorbonne in Paris. Since 1969 he has served as African Affairs editor for

Encyclopedia Britannica. Irvine's book is filled with positive comments regarding Blacks in ancient history. He approvingly quotes Herodotus on the "black skin and wooly hair" of the Egyptians. [23] He raised two questions, and lets Diodorus Siculus answer the first regarding whether or not Egypt spread its influence into the African continent; and second, whether or not Egypt drew heavily on older African traditions, "fashioning out of them a new synthesis." [24] Irvine confirms Diodorus' report that the Egyptian culture was derived from Kush[25], and Herodotus' testimony of the ethnicity of the Egyptians in the fifth century B.C. Irvine also reported on "the black Queen of Sheba" (or Sabaea) who ruled in the tenth century B.C. over the southern part of the Arabian peninsula [26]; and that Greeks obtained some proportion of their religion and knowledge of astronomy from either Kush or Ethiopia (or both) through Egypt.[27] Septimus Severus, Emperor of Rome from A.D. 193-211, was said to be partially black African in origin (born in Tripolitania)[28]; and "among the Christians a most notable African was Saint Augustine, himself a Berber, who was born in Carthage." [29]

Irvine wrote that during the Byzantium period (455 A.D.-1453) and the middle ages (500-1500 A.D.) when Byzantium, Damascus and Baghdad represented the centers of world civilization, the medieval church maintained biblical truth and taught that all mankind, descended from Adam and later Noah. Observable racial differences were explained by the fact that some were descended from Shem, some of Ham, and some of Japheth. Later commentators connected Shem with Asia, Ham with Africa and Japheth with Europe. [30] Irvine claimed that, "so mixed, indeed was the blood of the Byzantines that racial prejudices were virtually non existent."[31] Irvine quoted Ibn Battuta, a fourteenth century Berber writer regarding the African kingdom south of the Sahara; he reported:

> Perfect security reigns: one may live and travel without fear of theft or rapine. They do not confiscate the goods of those white men who die in their country; even when they place the heritage in the keeping of curators chosen from amongst the white men. [32]

The International Standard Bible Encyclopedia also made comment about inner or central Africa in its discussion of Noah's son "Ham."

> Recent studies of African history reveals the existence in central Africa of a high level of civilization probably nurtured by the posterity of Ham. [33]

The prophet Jeremiah had no qualms relating Ethiopians to blackness (Jer. 13:23). The great English preacher, C.H. Spurgeon, in a sermon entitled "The Ethiopian" stated Jeremiah had a friend who was a black man. [34]

G. Campbell Morgan, commenting on the Ethiopian Eunuch in Acts 8:26-40 made the following comment:

...Probably he was indeed a man of Ethiopia in the full sense of the word, a son of Africa, himself one of the race of Ham, a negro. That is my own personal conviction. I believe he was the first of the African race to become a Christian. It is now established that at least three centuries before Christ, Greek literature and thought had permeated that central African district, and that a most remarkable civilization was realized under Candace... The Egyptian portraiture of the Ethiopians shows the distinct negro type. [35]

G. Campbell Morgan certainly considered descendants of Ham in Scripture to be Negroes.

Hal Lindsey, who is best known as author of *The Late Great Planet Earth* believes that Ham's son Cush was the father of all the black races. Lindsey states that "Moses' second wife was definitely Black". [36]

Martin Bernal, a professor at Cornell University in his book *Black Athena: The Afroasiatic Roots of Classical Civilization*, reveals,

...many modern scholars maintain that, while the biblical name Kus [Kush] generally referred to Nubia or Ethiopia, it was also used for two other regions and their people: The Midianites in Western Arabia and the Kassu or Kassites to the east of Mesopotamia who controlled Mesopotamia for much of the middle of the second millennium... [37]

Bernal further states:

...in fact there seem to have been two independent, similar names. In both cases, however, they would seem to have been for dark or black people. Thus, Kus [Kush] became a generic title for them. In this way, it was used for the darker Midianites to the southeast of Canaan, many of whom, like the South Arabians of today, resembled Somalis and other Northeast Africans. [38]

Dr. Walter Bruggemann of Columbia Seminary makes an acquiescing comment regarding the current effort by Black scholars to discover our biblical heritage.

We are discovering what we thought was objective scholarship really turns out to be white scholarship that is very much limited by our cultural categories and cultural horizons. [39]

Regarding the ethnicity of Jesus, Bruggemann stated, "It will not do for white Westerners to think of Christ as a white Westerner, which all our art has done, because he could not have been a white Westerner." [40]

John D. Morris, Ph.D., of the Institute For Creation Research, in Santee, California, responded to the question, "Where did the races come from?"

"Actually, the biblical model regarding the origin of physical characteristics is easily the best historical and scientific explanation. Starting with Noah's family, the creation model postulates a "racially mixed" population, with much biological potential for variation. As family groups were isolated by language barriers, environmental factors allowed particular traits already present to be expressed more frequently, while genes coded for other characteristics were not favored and were eventually suppressed. Genetically speaking, the difference between the various races are extremely small. All are of the same species, are interfertile, and produce fertile offspring. The most noticeable difference is in skin color, but the fact is, we are all the same color; some people just have a little more of that color than others. Skin shade is due to the amount of a substance called melanin in the skin; the more melanin, the darker the skin. Racially mixed individuals can parent children who are all the way from quite dark to quite light, or anywhere in between. The predominant shade for freely inter-breeding individuals would be brown.

While prejudice, persecution, and racial hatred follow directly from the application of evolutionary teaching, some have proposed racism in the name of Christianity. The Christian must not allow himself or herself to think this way. The Lord Jesus Christ certainly didn't. He was likely neither white nor black, but somewhere in between. [41]

Phillip Yancey, biblical scholar and editor of The Student Bible, the largest selling Bible in the United States, said that Solomon's mother was probably Black. Solomon was an ancestor of Jesus, Yancey added. [42]

Raymond H. Woolsey authored a marvelous work entitled, *Men and Women of Color in the Bible*. Woolsey records that "most of the biblical characters–including Jesus Christ–were probably of a darker complexion than the average European or other Westerner today." [43] The cover comment of Woosley's work describe his book as, "The intriguing yet factual story of the contribution made by people of Hamitic descent to the purposes of God on earth, as recorded in the pages of Holy Scriptures." [44] Ham and his children had a color identity before the so called curse of Ham episode according to Woolsey. He develops the Hamitic lineage in Scripture discussing their pigmentation and their participation in the biblical world. We regard Woolsey's discourse as the second most important contribution (behind Custance) by a White author regarding the presence of Blacks in the Bible.

The English scholar Joseph McCabe made a startling statement regarding superficial theories about race and ancient ethnicity:

> The accident of the predominance of white men in modern times should not give us supercilious ideas about color or persuade us to listen to superficial theories about the innate superiority of the white-skinned man. Four thousand years ago, when civilization was already one or two thousand years old, white men were just a bunch of semi-savages on the outskirts of the civilized world. If there had been anthropologists in Crete, Egypt, and Babylonia, they would have pronounced the white race obviously inferior, and might have discoursed learnedly on the superior germ-plasm or glands of colored folk. [45]

McCabe's view of history is rarely repeated. Moreover, since Genesis 10 is an accurate record of ancient ethnicity, it clearly informs us that Crete, Egypt and Babylonia descended from the family of Ham. It is without question that people of color have made significant contributions to the biblical and ancient world. This fact is virtually seldom discussed in White colleges, seminaries and local churches. Yet we are often asked, "What difference does it make regarding the color of people in scripture?"

We firmly believe that if the White evangelical church were to teach the ethnic history recorded in Genesis 10, along with all its implications throughout the history of Scripture we would see a great healing in Christianity that would impact the world. We believe such knowledge is capable of changing the misinformed attitudes of some Whites and serve to alleviate resentment felt by some Blacks.

We have seen in the preceding chapter that many White scholars do not believe that Blacks have a "history worth mentioning." Consequently, they have led many Whites to form the same conclusion. By denying, limiting, and ignoring the Black presence in Scripture, the White Christian community has contributed, intentionally or unintentionally, to racism in America. However, this can be corrected if the White community simply incorporate Genesis 10 into their teaching and accordingly acknowledge the Black presence in Scripture.

We are grateful to God for using J. Vernon McGhee, Arthur Custance, Raymond Woolsey, Count Volney, Keith Irvine, Herodotus, Diodorus Siculus, and others who have been willing to set the record straight and testify of the truth that God "hath made of one blood all nations of men for to dwell on all the face of the earth, and hath determined the times before appointed, and the bounds of their habitation." Acts 17:24. It is our prayer that this message would penetrate the White Christian community resulting in a profound, positive impact, not only on Christian education, but on evangelism, cross cultural fellowship, and society at large. It is also our desire that God use this message in redeeming the time (Ephesians 5:16).

NOTES
CHAPTER 3

1. J. Vernon McGhee, Through the Bible - Genesis, Thomas Nelson, Inc., Nashville, TN, 1981, p. 51.

2. Arthur C. Custance, Noah's Three Sons, Zondervan Corporation, Grand Rapids, MI, 1975, pp. 13-1, 72, 122-123, 152, 201.

3. C.F. Keil and F. Kelitzsch, Commentary on the Old Testament, Hendrickson Publishers, Inc., Peabody, MA, Vol. 1, p. 164.

4. Ibid., p. 164.

5. Morris A. Gutstein, "Ham", Colliers Encyclopedia, MacMillan Educational Co., 1991, p. 603.

6. Quoted by St. Clair Drake in Black Folk Here and There, Center for Afro-American Studies, University of California, Los Angeles, 1987, Vol. I, p. 133. See Diop, Cheikh Anta, The African Origin of Civilization. Translated from French by Mercer Cook, Lawrence Hill & Company, Westport, pp. 27-28, and Volney, Count Constatin De. Voyages en Syrie et en Egypte, Paris, 1787.

7. Ibid.

8. Herodotus. Herodotus: The Histories, A. de Selincourt, trans. London: Penguin, pp. 104-105, quoted by Martin Bernal, Black Athena, Vol. II, The Archaeological and Documentary Evidence, Rutgers University Press, New Brunswick, NJ, 1991, pp. 248-249.

9. John Skinner, A Critical and Exegetical Commentary on Genesis: The International Critical Commentary, T&T Clark Ltd., Edinburgh, Scotland, pp. 200-201.

10. A.H. Sayce, The Races of the Old Testament World, The Religious Tract Society, London and Tonbridge, 1925, pp. 42-43.

11. Ibid., p. 60-61.

12. Ibid., pp. 60-61.

13. H. G. Wells, A Short History of the World, London: Heinemann, 1927, p. 59.

14. John F. Walvoord, The Nations, Israel and the Church in Prophecy. Academie Books, Zondervan Publishing House, Grand Rapids, Michigan, 1988, p. 26.

15. Ibid., p. 29.

16. Ibid., p. 25.

17. Ibid., pp. 31-32.

18. Ibid., pp. 31-32.

19. Ibid., pp. 32, 33.

20. Ibid., p. 165.

21. .Pat Roberson, Answers to 200 of Life's Most Probing Ques-

tions, Thomas Nelson Publishers, Nashville, 1984, p. 56.

22. Keith Irvine, The Rise of the Colored Races, W.W. Norton & Company, New York, 1970, p. 32.

23. I bid., p. 10.

24. Ibid., p. 10.

25. Ibid., p. 12.

26. Ibid., p. 14.

27. Ibid., p. 15.

28. Ibid., p. 19.

29. Ibid., p. 19.

30. Ibid., p. 21.

31. Ibid., pp. 25-26.

32. Ibid., p. 32.

33. "Ham", The International Standard Bible Encyclopedia, William B. Eerdmans Publishing Company, Grand Rapids, MI, 1988, Vol. 2, p. 601.

34. C. H. Spurgeon, "The Ethiopian," The Searchlight, September 1989, p. 1.

35. G. Campbell Morgan, The Acts of the Apostles, Fleming H. Revell Company, Old Tappan, NJ, 1924, p. 213.

36. Hal Lindsey, Combat Faith, Bantam Books, New York, 1986, p. 87.

37. Martin Bernal, Black Athena: The Afroasiatic Roots of Classical Civilization, Vol. II, The Archaeological and Documentary Evidence, Rutgers University Press, New Brunswick, NJ, 1991, p. 253.

38. Ibid., p. 253.

39. Gayle White, "Scholars: Africa's Role In Bible Ignored - But Blacks Getting Their Point Across," The Atlanta Journal, Religious Section, January 26, 1991.

40. Judith Lynn Howard, "Black Scholars Challenge Traditional Portrayals of Jesus," The Dallas Morning News, May 1, 1993, p. 42A.

41. John D. Morris, "Where Did the Races Come From?" The Torch, Vol. 3, No. 4, Fall Issue 1992, p. 1.

42. Monica Copeland, "Author on Mission to Reclaim Blacks' Heritage in the Bible," Chicago Tribune, March 8, 1991, p. 8., Section 2.

43. Raymond H. Woolsey, "Men and Women of Color in the Bible," International Bible, Inc., Langley Park, MD, 1977, Special Section, p. 5, cited in The Holy Bible, Authorized King James Version, Heritage Edition, Stampley Enterprises, Inc., Charlotte, NC, 1977.

44. Ibid., p. 1.

45. Joseph McCabe, "Life Among the May Peoples of the Earth, p. 26, quoted by John G. Jackson, Introduction to African Civilizations, The Citadel Press, Secaucus, NJ, 1970, p. 78.

Chapter 4

REDEFINING WHO WE ARE

The success and widespread interest in Alex Haley's *ROOTS*, proves that there is an innate curiosity in most of us as to our ancestors. In recent years there has been an increased number of books, tapes, and conferences on the subject of the Black presence in Scripture. Our purpose is to examine the viewpoints of Black biblical scholars and major contributions of the Black community on the matter of racial diversity in Scripture. Additionally, we want to make a passionate appeal for Black churches to incorporate the study of Blacks In The Bible into their Christian education curriculum. It is the responsibility of our Black churches to take the lead in this study. We can no longer leave it to White churches and White academia to objectively evaluate the Scriptures as it relates to racial diversity. This chapter will introduce many resources from Black writers and speakers that will aid the Black church in developing a study of Blacks in the Bible.

There are four reasons why it is important to study biblical ethnicity:

■ ...because the Bible is the inerrant, infallible, authoritative Word of God, it is the only place we can go to receive a totally accurate and objective understanding of race.

■ Rooting racial history and culture in the Bible allows us to contradict those who would write off the Bible as a White man's book. When a person understands the glorious presence of African people in God's drama of the unfolding of human history in general and redemptive history in particular, it becomes clear that Scripture should be the primary source of legitimate Black pride.

■ Since race has played such a major role in social development and the functioning of American society, it behooves one to discover the divine response to attempts at victimization based on race. This was the problem Moses faced when his sister Miriam and brother Aaron rebelled against him for marrying a Cushite, an African woman (Num.12)....Knowing that God rejected social rebellion based on racist attitude is instructional for both White and Black people who allow racial decisions to determine social and political structures in America.

■ A study of race rooted in the Bible links the pride and understanding of

Redefining Who We Are 55

race with an eternal purpose....When it is seen that the very lineage of Jesus included Blacks and that the leadership of the first century church included Africans, then African-Americans can take pride in the fact that we are an integral part of God's redemptive agenda and have played a decisive role in disseminating that agenda to the rest of the world. [1]

Rev. Walter McCray in his book THE BLACK PRESENCE IN THE BIBLE points out:

From a Christian viewpoint it is important for Black people to understand their Biblical history. Understanding the Black presence within the Bible nurtures among Black people an affection for the Scriptures and the things of the Lord. [2]

Carter G. Woodson founder of *Negro History Week* argued, "If a race has no history, it has no worthwhile tradition, it becomes a negligible factor in the thought of the world, and it stands in danger of being exterminated," [3] This statement was made in support of the observance of Negro History Week, but also holds true for the history of Blacks in the Bible.

Taking a flight off Woodson's runway, Anthony T. Browder goes a step further expressing the belief that the study of ancient Black biblical history not only vindicates our past, but is capable of having a profound and positive impact upon our present-day predicament.

We must be very mindful of the fact that just one hundred and fifty years ago, African Americans were still slaves. By law, we were forbidden from learning to read or write. The reasons were very obvious. 'Information is power.' Information holds the key to freedom from mental and physical bondage.... If you deny any people the knowledge of their history and culture, you deny them the ability to develop to their full potential. It is the responsibility of every adult to know their history and culture, to preserve it and then pass it on to the next generation. [4]

The subject of Blacks in the Bible has been affirmatively addressed (but with very limited exposure) by Blacks in America from the 1700's without interruption. Yet, it is apparent that only within the past five years has this fact made major inroads into the consciousness and curriculums of many Black churches. However, there still remains a muddle of skepticism, apathy, neutrality and resistance by many pastors and churches toward the Black participation in Scripture. The Black Muslim Community, segments of Black academia, and quasi Black cult groups have "preached" the prominence of Blacks in ancient history for years, often citing the Bible as its main reference while mainstream Black evangelical pastors and churches remained silent on the issue. Oftentimes, some Black evangelical leaders spoke against the relevance or prominence of Blacks in the Bible and in the ancient world. The majority of Black America has been innocently ignorant or romantically sympathetic on the matter until recent years.

Most Black churches celebrate Black History Month, but the focus is usually on Black American History because there is very little awareness or appreciation for Black Biblical History. We believe that every predominately Black church must equip their congregations by providing biblical, historically accurate and logical answers to the relevance and value of their ancestral presence in Scripture.

The Black church must prepare herself to address the following questions: Where did Black people come from? Is it an accurate and honest portrayal of history to depict all Bible characters as European? Are the images of European Bible characters hanging on walls and portrayed in Sunday School books in most Black churches a result of objective historical research that has led to that conclusion or do the pictures represent the unfounded bias of the producer of the pictures? Are pictures of European Bible characters constantly depicted in Black churches psychologically unhealthy for Black youth, children and even adults? Are Black church leaders passively cooperating with and financing White academia and ecclesiastical racism when we accept these images without question? What is the message we send to Black people who are well read in ancient history and have concluded that people of color were politically, numerically and culturally dominant in the ancient world up until the time of Alexander the Great, but yet all biblical historical pictures prior to that time reflect Europeans?

We are losing many of our young men and women, strong in body and mind, to Black Muslims and other non-Christian groups who are attempting to provide them answers to the question of the historical and religious significance of Black people. Our contemporary generation will no longer accept neutral or racist answers to the issues of blackness. These INQUIRING MINDS WANT TO KNOW! And if the church does not tell them, they either remain in darkness or often seek answers from those who do not believe in our Christ or our Bible. The question is how will we respond? The Bible says,

> But sanctify the Lord God in your hearts: and be ready always to give an answer to every man that asketh you a reason of the hope that is in you, with meekness and fear. (I Pet.3:15 KJV)

Peter taught that Christians should always respond with rational and respectful answers to every one that ask about our faith in Christ. If those who are disinterested in this information never avail themselves to this information, we will not be able to obey Peter's admonition and provide answers to those who ask questions related to Christianity and race. Many people will not accept the response that race is a non-issue or it doesn't matter. INQUIRING MINDS WANT TO KNOW! Our family, friends, neighbors, co-workers, children or someone will inevitably one day broach this subject with us. We need to be READY TO GIVE AN ANSWER. Eternal life for someone may hinge upon our response.

In addition to the previous questions listed, we believe every Black Christian ought to be prepared to answer the following questions: What Bible character had three descendants to settle on African soil? Where was the garden of Eden? Who was the father of darkest complexioned people in Scripture? How did Ham get his complexion? Were Blacks ever cursed in Scripture? What role did Africans play in the New Testament and post--New Testament Christianity? What color was Jesus? What was the role and identity of the Black man in ancient history? INQUIRING MINDS WANT TO KNOW! We believe that any church who fails to provide answers to these basic questions to Black believers are woefully remiss in their responsibilities of dealing faithfully with the whole council of God.

We certainly can relate to those who feel as if this subject matter is unimportant and irrelevant. As previously stated, that was my posture at one point. We can also relate to those who feel like this information should not be used as an attempt to heighten self esteem. We basically agree: If a Black Christian's self esteem is raised, it ought to be as a by-product of this information. The Christian's self esteem should come from the cross. The Apostle Paul said, "God forbid that I should glory save in the cross of the Lord Jesus Christ" (Gal. 6:14). However, just as all ethnic groups celebrate their history, culture and heritage, we believe Blacks ought to celebrate ours and realize that we have a history that goes beyond Shaka Zulu and Kunta Kente. Our history goes back to Genesis--the book of beginnings. "In the beginning was the Word and the Word was with God and the Word was God. The same was in the beginning with God. All things were made by Him and without Him was not anything made that was made" (John 1:1,2). Our history goes back to the beginning when God made man.

We do believe that this message should be used to refute the teaching handed down from one generation to another in modern history that Blacks are innately inferior to other races. What better witness can we call to the stand to testify about the Black man other than God who said that the Ethiopians (descendants of Ham) were great from their beginning (Is. 18:1-2).

Although we obviously believe that the most important use of this message (Blacks In The Bible) is to serve an evangelistic and apologetic (defense of the faith) objective. We also believe this message should be used in Christian education and cultural celebration.

Perhaps Dr. E.V. Hill of Los Angeles, summarizes the sentiments of those who limit the use of this message to an evangelistic or apologetic objective in a message he preached at the Concord Baptist Church in Dallas at their Annual Joy Explosion in August 1985. The title of the message was "AND GOD MADE MAN" (Gen. 1:27). Specifically Dr. Hill is commenting on Alex Haley's writing (ROOTS), and the movie that reveals Haley's apparent belief that the Blacks who came to America from Africa during slavery were Islamic. Hill's lengthy response to Alex Haley in his message is printed here almost in its entirety. Along the way he inadvertently shares brief insights of his views regarding Blacks in the Bible, ancient history, the spread of Islam and why Black people fell from political and educational prominence, and why White people were elevated. Hill declared:

> Mr. Alex Haley in his book ROOTS led to much confusion by suggesting that we are a people of original Islamic faith. He had in his book and in the play where the slaves were calling on the name Allah, referring to the Islamic God. But Mr. Haley's book stopped in the eleventh century. He didn't go back far enough. Anybody who does not understand that Christianity invaded Africa the first century, I give you an "F" in history. When you speak of Egypt and Ethiopia, when you speak of Alexandria, when you speak of the great cities of the book of Acts, you're in Africa. He was born in brown Asia. He fled to Black Africa. And he was back in heaven before the gospel got to White Europe. Now does that make Him black? No. Does that make Him brown? No. As a matter of fact anyone who bows at the cross and get up with color on his mind needs to bow again. When you bow at the cross and raise your head and the burden rolls away, you get up with Jesus on your mind. And so, I dare not spend a moment talking about the blackness of Jesus, because He is whatever color he has to be. He's a white man's best friend. He's the black man's deliverer. He's the brown man's hope. He's everything. Mr. Donahue along with Alex Haley would have Negroes believe we started out with Islam. Islam started in the sixth century. Jesus was in Africa the first century. What happened is very simple and I trust you know. When Mohammed came to Africa and said to Africans give up the cross or I thrust the sword, that Negro looked at the sword and he looked at the cross and he said 'don't be no fool.' And Mohammed con-quered Africa by the sword not by the Bible...You just have to let the chips fall where they may. You cannot mess with truth, if you're

interested in history. And so he caused all Africa to turn from Jesus and the true God and bow to the East with the threat of the sword. When he got to White Europe he said to the white folks, 'the sword or the cross.' And the white folks said 'the sword. We'd rather die than to give up the cross.' See how quiet you all got. But that's a part of history. And God gave them strength to whip him back into Africa where we accepted him. The results of which is when he came to us we were Kings, the cradle of civilization and Europe was almost in heathenism. But as they accepted Christ they rose. And as we rejected Him we failed. Have you all ever wondered how we went from education to bone head? We were the cradle of civilization. How did we fall from the top of education to running around with bones in our head. Any man who rejects Christ becomes a bonehead....It was in the fourteenth century when they put us on boats ...and brought us over here and we were not introduced to Christianity, we were reintroduced to Christianity. That's how we took it away from them so fast. White folks had it and didn't know what to do with it and as soon as we got it we said "Steal Away To Jesus, Ain't Got Long To Stay Here." Now that's our history and we must accept that before we can move on with God. [5]

Dr. Hill's comments embrace the view of the prominence of Blacks at an early point in history and a Black presence in Scripture. His comments also sound a clear warning against emphasizing color in Christianity. Hill's main point and the only reason he voiced his views were to rebuke the popular teaching in the Black community that Islam is the natural religion of the Black man. He adequately and eloquently refutes that position. The subject of Blacks in the Bible is extremely important and must be taught in our churches if we are to equip our people to refute the Muslims claim. Hill's comments reflect the view that the White man has not always "been on top" in world history.

Mainstream sacred or secular academia has never taught that the great people of ancient history were people of color. This we believe is a terrible mistake and partly responsible for the poor race relations in this country. If the truth sets us free, Black people have never been taught the truth about our history in most public classrooms. Therefore, many Blacks have not been set free from bitterness regarding institutional and systemic racism in America. One reason the church must teach these truths is because the Eurocentric dominated school system is not going to do it. And until these truths are taught, we believe many of our people will be gripped by the same racist demon that has gripped many White people as evidenced by the increased acts of racial violence throughout our nation. We truly believe that if this information is shared within the context of other Christian truths in our main line churches in every city and hamlet and village across America and spread into the "psyches" of most Black Americans it will greatly reduce the odds of our cities going up in smoke like Los Angeles did in '92. We will fight back intellectually, legally, economically, prayerfully and in every other nonviolent legal and sensible manner, but the truth will have set us free from the senseless violence and anarchy that have many of our people gripped.

Black churches that have failed to teach about race from the Bible have unknowingly contributed to the rejection of Christianity, especially by our youth. The major attraction that our youth have toward gangs and the Black Muslims is partly driven by the fact that the gangs and the Black Muslims address issues related to race while the church is often silent. According to the scholarly Southern California pastor Chuck Singleton, "Malcolm X was embittered by racism and turned to the Black Muslims because they gave expression to his rage."[6] If the Black Christian church had taught truths about the glorious past of Blacks in the Bible and did not give room to pictures of White Bible characters on its walls, they may have won Malcolm X. We can only imagine how effective Malcolm X may have been as a Christian evangelist, preaching the gospel of Blacks in the Bible. He would have related to Blacks who ordinarily would not have identified with Christianity because of the perception that Christianity is a White man's religion and were repelled by Bible characters depicted as Whites. A voice like Malcolm's could have used this information as a bridge to share with Blacks the true message of Christianity and probably would have had an evangelistic appeal and ministry such as the scope of Billy Graham's. But only God knows best.

In Adam Clayton Powell's autobiography *ADAM by ADAM* he discussed how he once shared with Malcolm X the fact that Christianity was not the White man's Religion and the Ethiopians were committed Christians prior to the Europeans.[7] Adam Powell had a vast understanding of Ethiopian history. The church he pastored was named "Abyssinian Baptist Church." Abyssinian is a synonym for Ethiopia. Powell also earned his Masters in Religious Education from Columbia University. We, too, can use this truth (Ethiopians were Christians before Europeans) to aggressively win fellow Blacks to the faith.

Dr. Cain Hope Felder, in his book *TROUBLING BIBLICAL WATERS* has given the subject of Blacks in the Bible an academic acceptability and credibility among many mainline Black churches. Dr. Felder stated that hundreds of Black Muslim inmates have written him letters renouncing Islam and turning to Christ because his writings accurately refuted the erroneous but popular belief that Islam is the natural religion of the Black man.[8] Black churches who refuse to teach about the Black biblical presence are ill equipping their members to obey the scriptural admonition to be ready to give answers to others who ask about and challenge our faith in Christ (1 Peter 3:15). However, we cannot compromise the inerrant Word of God for the sake of cultural identity.

Dr. Eddie Lane, a professor at Dallas Theological Seminary, in response to a news reporter's question regarding the book *TROUBLING BIBLICAL WATERS* stated:

> In his pursuit of establishing a spiritual heritage of Blacks, all the way back to Africa--which is fine and we all like that--the problem is that his conclusions are very, very dangerous because he denounces the biblical text. I found this book to be a very dangerous threat to Black evangelicals and Black evangelism. My fear is that his historical emphasis on blackness will cause us to forgive his liberal view of the Bible. [9]

In addressing his popular class on evangelism at the National Baptist Congress of Christian Education held in Oklahoma City in June, 1991 Dr. Manuel L. Scott, Sr. sounded a cautionary alarm in a message entitled "*THE CHURCH IN CHRIST'S PERSPECTIVE.*"

> In collision and competition with the true church is the Ethnic Model....It is not a sinful or futile endeavor now being put forth by Black scholars and others to identify Jesus' origins in the flesh with those of Black descent. It may energize our Evangelism and enlist some Blacks who otherwise would not camp with us. Nevertheless, we must not allow any current `Black Manifestos' to inspire a dual anthropology, Christology and bring to pass what Paul Tillich once feared -`racism in reverse.' The church must continue to contend as Martin Luther King so eloquently preached `it is the content of one's character, rather than the color of his skin' that is most critical for his earthly and eternal destiny. We must make sure that the liturgies, rituals, sermons, songs, politics and general tone and tenor, communicate that we offer a salvation in Jesus Christ that is, unmistakably, cosmopolitan. The truth of the gospel is that Christ died to save all races. [10]

Unfortunately, there are some Black scholars who deny the historicity of Genesis 1-11 and the literal approach to Scriptural interpretation in general. Consequently, while leaving their readers impressed with identifying a Black presence in Scripture, they run the risk of leaving them unimpressed with the integrity of Scripture as a whole. This can be quite damaging as Dr. Lane points out. While they exalt ethnicity, they deny the inerrancy of Scripture and salvation only through the shed blood of Jesus.

They then make it possible to leave their readers well educated regarding biblical and ancient ethnicity but ignorant of the efficacy of the evangel (Christ). Convincing people that there is a Black presence in Scripture without emphasizing or teaching the absolute authority of Scripture and the saving power of Jesus Christ borders on idolatry. Knowing that there is a Black presence in Scripture may enhance one's self esteem and knowledge of history, but this knowledge is absolutely of no value when it compares to eternal life. We seriously question the ultimate value of a message that exalts ethnicity and evades the Christ. One serious concern is that many who proudly wear kente cloth, Afro hairstyles and propagate biblical, Black, and ancient history may not see the glorified Jesus if we only bow to His mixed race and not to His righteousness and rulership over our lives regardless of race.

Dr. Kenneth Ulmer of Los Angeles, California in a message entitled "Biblical Black History" eloquently reminded us of the danger of "ethnicizing" Deity.

> Any attempts to ethnicize Deity will by definition imply a civil war within the family. If, in fact, I make my God Black then what does that do to my yellow brother, or my brown brother. It does not validate my White brother's attempt to make God and Christ White....God in His essence transcends color....God is too big to be limited to my Blackness, but He is to loving to forget about my Blackness. [11]

An African Connection

David Tuesday Adamo, a native of Africa, attended Baylor University in 1986 and for his dissertation submitted *The Place of Africa and Africans in the Old Testament Environment.* Adamo stated:

> This investigator establishes the fact that Africa and Africans have made an enormous contribution to the entire life of the ancient Near East, particularly ancient Israel....A significant part of that contribution is suggested by the strong possibility of African origin of the Sumerian and Egyptian religions. [12]

Adamo also identified Ebedmelech, the Queen of Sheba, Jehudi and the Kushite among David's soldiers, as Africans. He also highlights the military and political contribution of Africa and Africans to the people of the ancient Near East 13 during the Cushite dynasty. Perhaps Adamo's greatest contribution is the argument that the Garden of Eden was in Africa (PP. 78-96). Adamo went on to claim that Zephaniah was of African ancestry (P.261) and Hezekiah trusted and depended on African might and power (Is. 18:1-2,7; 20:1-6; II Kings 19:8-19) as one of Israel's allies.

Dr. Charles Copher published his first article on the Black presence in Scripture in 1970. Copher, a distinguished and eminent scholar of the Old Testament and Professor Emiritus of Old Testament at the Interdenominational Theological Center of Atlanta, Ga. earned a Ph.D. in Old Testament Studies from Boston University. Dr. Copher's writings appear in *STONY THE ROAD WE TROD* edited by Cain Hope Felder, *Nile Valley Civilizations,* and *African Presence in Early Asia,* edited by Ivan Van Sertima of Rutgers University. In his writings, Copher classifies Abraham, Zephaniah, Cushi, the Egyptians, Ethiopians and Elamites, Phineas, Chushan - Rishathaim (Jud. 3:7-10) and the Queen of Sheba as Black. [14]

Copher's writings represent a vast amount of technical, critical and scholarly information. We understand from Dr. Copher that the discussion of Blacks in the Bible began in the year 1742 by Jacob Elisa Capitein (1717-1742). This discussion was rekindled in 1760 by Jupiter Hammond[15] and continued uninterrupted to the present. Although those of us who preach the message of Blacks in the Bible are sometimes accused of preaching something new, to which we answer, "If it's new, it's not true; and if it's true, it's not new." Solomon said, "there is nothing new under the sun." The origin of Blacks was first seen in Genesis chapter ten. Copher made the following noteworthy comment regarding those who recorded views on Blacks in the Bible.

> In reviewing publications by Black writers from 1837 to 1962, one notes that with few exceptions every Black writer dealt with a glorious, ancient Black history based upon the Bible which was viewed as factual. Thus, so spoke and wrote the Reverend H. Easton in 1837; James C. Pennington in 1841; R.B. Lewis in 1844; Henry H. Garnett in 1848; Martin R. Delany in 1952; Alexander Crumwell in 1862; William Wells Brown again in 1874; George Washington Williams in 1883; Edward A. Johnson in 1891; Rufus L. Perry in 1893; Benjamin T. Tanner in 1902; and J.J. Pipkin in 1902. All these were Afro-Americans; all were traditionalist in their view of the Bible. Interestingly enough the works of Perry and Tanner were written partly to refute the Hamite doctrine that removed Blacks from the Bible. [16]

Rev. Walter Arthur McCray of Chicago, Illinois published *THE BLACK PRESENCE IN THE BIBLE* VOLUMES I and II in 1990. The studies were written from a conservative viewpoint designed to equip the reader to discover the Black and African identity of biblical persons and nations. McCray makes an interesting comment with regard to a degree of blackness within the Semitic genealogical line:

...the ancient Biblical Semites contained a marked degree of blackness within their genealogical line. To cite a few instances, see 'Elam,' 'Asshur,' and 'Lud,' 'Sheba' and 'Havilah' in Shem's genealogical line (Genesis 10:22, 28, 29). Historically, in addition to Hamite Blacks, there has existed Asiatic Blacks including Semite Blacks. Furthermore, let us beware of the flawed thinking which tells us that the biblical covenant people were not Black or White but `Jews.' To assert for the sake of a color and/or ethnological argument that the biblical covenant community were `Jews" says no more about their precise anthropological/ethnological composition and appearance relative to their Black kindredness than our saying that they were `Semitic' or `Semites.' [17]

As a matter of fact, we agree that the children of Israel must have been heterogeneous with respect to ethnicity. That is, those who considered themselves to be part of Israel, must have borne a range of skin colors. We must remember that the claim of Jacob's inheritance was not a matter of skin color but rather a matter of lineage. Manasseh and Ephraim were born to Joseph while he was in Egypt, yet Jacob (Israel) made it very clear in Genesis 48:5 that Manasseh and Ephraim were to be treated as sons. Therefore, they were to receive an inheritance in the 'Promised Land.' Thus, it is probable that the Nubian stock entered the line of Israel at this juncture.

The writer of the preface for *THE ORIGINAL AFRICAN HERITAGE STUDY BIBLE* (published by Winston Derik Publishers, a Black owned publishing company of Nashville, Tenn.) took a radical departure from most Black scholars who have written on the subject of Blacks in the Bible and from the basic teaching of the church regarding racial origins from 500-1500 A.D. The writer denied that the sons of Noah represented three races.

> ...the sons of Noah—Shem, Ham, and Japheth—do not represent three different races. (It is an absurdity of no small order to claim that Noah and his wife could produce offspring that would constitute three distinct racial types!)...Furthermore, Ham does not mean "black" in Hebrew; it translates literally as "hot" or "heated". It does not make sense to say, logically or scientifically, that within the ten generations from Adam to Noah (and without the introduction of any outside factors), a genetic change took place which allowed one man (Noah) and his one wife (of the same race as himself) to produce children who were racially different! This is the logic many would have the modern reader believe. [18]

We are in full disagreement with the conclusive argument that

Ham's ethnicity is based on the etymology of his name. We will set forth our argument in the next chapter.

Furthermore, we disagree with the writer's claim that it is illogical or unscientific to equate that Noah and his wife were incapable of producing distinct racial types. It is contrary to mainstream Black deliberation and the Bible's categorical classification of all people on the face of the earth according to their biological kinship to Noah's sons (Gen. 9:19; 10:1,6,20,21,31). If the physical features of persons classified according to Noah's three sons is studied, they will obviously constitute three different races. We will address in detail in the next chapter the logic and scientific reasoning behind Black evangelicals' viewpoint that Noah's sons do represent three different races and that Ham was the father of the Black race. However, in spite of our disagreement in this area, we highly recommend that those interested in this subject matter avail themselves of the wealth of information found in *THE ORIGINAL AFRICAN HERITAGE STUDY BIBLE.*

The late great Baptist preacher C.L. Franklin of Detroit, to some degree echoes the view regarding Noah's sons recorded in *THE ORIGINAL AFRICAN HERITAGE STUDY BIBLE.* Jeff Todd Titon edited a book entitled *GIVE ME THIS MOUNTAIN*, published by the University of Illinois Press in 1989. Todd's book contains the life history, interviews and twenty selected sermons by Clarence Lavaughn Franklin. Todd simply transferred Franklin's messages from "wax" to print. Franklin used the text Genesis 9:20-28 under the caption "The Preacher Who Got Drunk":

> In this particular story, frequently it is used by segregationist as an example of why the Negro is black. They make Ham the ancient ancestor of black people, and of course, they make the other sons, Shem and Japheth, the ancestors of other racial groups. ...Ham is not the ancient ancestor of black people. And black people are not black because God cursed them because Ham saw his father drunk and naked. ...I'm sure that there were Black people way before Ham. ...man did not come to racial characteristics, color, etcetera, by somebody's curse. ...If man came from the ground, you understand, it seems like original man couldn't have been white. ...You know, out of the dust of the ground, God created us? So "atoma," from which our word atom comes, means earth. Now who has ever seen any white earth? ...And, of course, the Bible says a certain situation arose and Moses' hand turned white. Now if Moses was already white, how did his hand turn white? Hunh? Nobody but somebody dark could have a white hand? [19]

Dr. Renita Weems is a professor of Old Testament at Vanderbilt

Divinity School in Nashville, Tennessee and earned her Ph.D in Old
Testament Studies from Princeton Theological Seminary. In her book
JUST A SISTER AWAY, she explained in a footnote the ethnic differences
between Hagar and Sarai in a chapter called "A Mistress, A Maid and No
Mercy", (Gen. 16: 1-16;21:1-21) Weems denotes:

> Certainly ancient people were aware of another's color (e.g. in Song
> of Solomon 1:5, the writer, presumably referring to her skin color as
> "dark and comely"; and in Numbers 12:10, it was as much that her
> skin turned 'white as snow' as it was that Miriam was a leper that
> the narrator felt deserved comment.) But there is no evidence that
> race and color, as we understand them today, especially as a way of
> stratifying people prevailed at the time. [20]

We know of no Black writer or speaker who embraces the traditional Eurocentric view of the so called "curse of Ham." We know of
Black lay persons who have expressed a belief in the "curse of Ham"
theory. There are Black South African pastors who had been taught the
"curse of Ham" theory by White Baptist professors in South Africa and
were never exposed to an alternative view. They believed the error until
they were exposed to the 'Beyond Roots I' discussion. If the Bible actually
taught the "curse of Ham" theory, those of us who share the fundamentalist approach to Scripture interpretation would be compelled to believe it.
Thank God that the Bible does not teach that Blacks have been cursed
through the erroneous curse of Ham theory.

Wayne Perryman is an eloquent and accurate spokesman on the
subject of Blacks in the Bible. His book *THOUGHT PROVOKING
BIBLE STUDIES OF THE 90's* is quite informative and inspirational.
However, we tend to differ with him on one point and that is his belief that
Canaan engaged in sexual relations with Noah's wife, and for that reason
Canaan was cursed and not Ham. In a message entitled, "The Case of The
Curse of Ham" at the Friendship Baptist Church in Yorba Linda, Ca. in
July 1993, Perryman in his attempt to vindicate Ham from the curse--
indicts Canaan. We agree that it was Canaan who was cursed and not
Ham but we do not believe that Canaan was cursed for the reasons men-
tioned by Perryman; yet, we certainly endorse Perryman's effort to refute
the curse of Ham theory.

Perryman has said that, "God Jehovah loved Ham and blessed all
of his descendants including Canaan. However, he eventually punished
Canaan because it was he who committed the horrible act on that day."
Perryman teaches that Noah and his wife had intercourse on that day of
Genesis 9:18-29 when Noah got drunk. After Noah had relations with his
wife he was still naked and young Canaan heard the commotion, so he

waited until his father fell asleep. "Young Canaan went in there and slept with his grandmother, and in the process of fornicating with his grandmother, his father Ham overheard it. Ham went in the tent and saw his son having sex with his grandmother, Ham's mother, Mrs. Noah...and he took Young Canaan out of the tent angry with the son for committing this act. As he was escorting his son out of the tent, he told his two brothers...I caught young Canaan having sex with Mom please go in there and cover her. ...It was young Canaan who committed the horrible act of having sex with Mrs. Noah and therefore uncovered his father's nakedness."[21]

Perryman based his belief that Canaan had sex with his grandmother, straining a correlation of Leviticus 18:7,8; 20:11 with the Genesis 9:18-20 text. Leviticus 18:7,8 and 20:11 reads as follows:

> The nakedness of thy father, or the nakedness of thy mother, shalt thou not uncover: she is thy mother; thou shalt not uncover her nakedness. The nakedness of thy father's wife shalt thou not uncover: it is thy father's nakedness. And the man that lieth with his father's wife hath uncovered his father's nakedness.... [22]

We assume since the curse was pronounced upon Canaan as opposed to Ham, Perryman concluded that Canaan must have looked upon "the nakedness of his father" (Gen. 9:22). However, the text clearly states that, "Ham, the father of Canaan, saw the nakedness of his father" (Gen. 9:22). Perryman referenced the Leviticus passage to extrapolate that seeing the "nakedness of the father" meant sleeping with the father's wife because "The nakedness of thy father's wife (Lev. 18:8). ... is thy father's nakedness" (Lev. 20:11). According to Perryman, if Canaan saw "the nakedness of his father" that meant he slept with his father's wife, and for that act the curse was pronounced upon him. [23]

Most theologians are familiar with the terms isogesis and exegesis. Isogesis is basically reading into the text what it does not declare. Exegesis is reading exactly what the text indicates. In our opinion, Perryman's view of the "curse of Canaan" is an extreme case of isogesis and it inadequately as well as inaccurately attempts to refute the "curse of Ham" theory. Even if Perryman's correlation and interpretation of the Leviticus passages are appropriately accurate, still, they would apply to Ham, not to Canaan. Why? Because Genesis 9:22 clearly states it was Ham who "saw the nakedness of his father."

We repeat, apart from Perryman's "curse of Canaan" theory, we have found his communication to be impressive and inspiring. We salute him for taking the Scriptures literally, but we responded to his view of the "curse" closely because he is the only Black man that we know of who holds this view of the curse. However, we read and listened to Whites with similar fallacious and isogetical viewpoints.

The great Black historian, W.E.B. Dubois revealed in his book *THE NEGRO* his belief that, "The biblical story of Shem, Ham, and Japheth retains the interest of a primitive myth with its measure of allegorical truth, but has, of course, no historical basis." [24] Dubois further claims, "It is sufficient to remember that for several centuries leaders of the Christian church gravely defended Negro slavery and oppression as the rightful curse of God upon the descendants of a son who had been disrespectful to his drunken father." [25] On the other hand, Bishop Alfred G. Dunston lays the blame at the feet of White scholars for many young Black Americans who now view the Bible as a White man's book. In the mid 70's, Dunston's book *THE BLACK MAN IN THE OLD TESTAMENT AND ITS WORLD* was the first enlightening study on the Black presence in Scripture. In the late 70's, seminary students commonly discussed Dr. Charles Copher's writings. Then in 1988 John Johnson's *THE BLACK BIBLICAL HERITAGE* became widely read and researched. Felder's *TROUBLING BIBLICAL WATERS* was another well referenced source of study. There was just not much in print on this subject in the 80's. Today, scores of books have been written on the subject. Dunston's book was first published in 1974 and has been recently republished (1992) by Africa World Press, Inc. of Trenton, New Jersey. When Dunston's book was first published he served as the Bishop of the African Methodist Episcopal Zion Church of America. In spite of the numerous publications, why do many well-read Black Americans hold the view that the Bible is still a White man's book? Dunston offers the following reason...

> Since the opening years of the sixteenth century, Christian biblical scholarship has been the ally of racism, sometimes deliberately and sometimes unconsciously. The alliance has run the gamut from avid support of the black inferiority myth to a mere indifference to the situation; and at both extremes, the racial myths have found growing room. In all likelihood there are millions of Christians today who still believe the curse of Noah fell upon the black man. This fallacy was once taught by leading white scholars and writers of their day, and the successors of those scholars and writers have done very little to erase the fallacy. Secular writers have done more to correct these myths than biblical ones; and this is possibly one of the reasons that many young Black Americans call the Holy Scripture 'the White man's Bible.' [26]

Since White scholars according to Dunston have done very little to erase the fallacy of Black inferiority or the curse of Ham theory, then it is incumbent upon Black scholars to address this issue.

Earnest C. Sargent III, in his book *MAJESTIC HONOR BIBLI-*

CAL PERSPECTIVES IN BLACK HISTORY eloquently articulates the spiritual impact and value that this subject holds for Blacks. Sargent writes, "...when we incorporate the beauty of the ethnic factor into our studies we find the Bible illuminated with a vivid clarity, striking color and true-to-life pictures that greatly enhance our understanding of God's Word and God's love."[27] Pastor Alvin Jones of Washington D.C., in his book *ROYALTY WITHOUT A FUTURE: RESTORING THE DEVASTATED HERITAGES* calls for all races to be reflected in portrayals of Biblical people.

> If you were to look at the average Bible, it lacks authenticity in regards to pictures of various races of people. From Adam in the Garden of Eden to John in Revelation, every nation, kindred, tongue, and people were used by God. From Italians to Greeks to Israelites to Ethiopians, each nation should be portrayed in the role that God intended for its people to be. [28]

Our bibliography will list many other books written by Blacks on this matter. Most of them underscores the viewpoint that Ham was Black and all his descendants listed in Genesis chapter ten were Black. In this chapter, we have labored to introduce the reader to books and tapes that we think are most insightful on the subject, to show diverse thinking on the subject in the Black Community, and to appeal to Black churches to include this subject matter into their Annual Church Calendars. We press even further to specifically recommend the following studies to those who wish to inquire extensively: Frank Snowden has written two books *BLACKS IN ANTIQUITY* and *BEFORE COLOR PREJUDICE* both published by Harvard University Press complete with illustrations from the ancient world which document that Blacks lived and traveled (throughout) all countries of the ancient world (Africa, Europe and the Middle East) and served in positions from slaves to Kings. The color of skin was clearly not the dominant issue until the Renaissance period.

St. Clair Drake, a retired Stanford Professor penned two volumes entitled *BLACK FOLK HERE AND THERE* Volumes I and II, where he discussed the prominence and place of Blacks in ancient and classical history. The following four books we highly recommend for those interested in the Black presence in the ancient world from a secular scholarly view point: *NILE VALLEY CIVILIZATIONS, AFRICAN PRESENCE IN EARLY ASIA and AFRICAN PRESENCE IN EARLY EUROPE*. These books were all edited by Ivan Van Sertima who is a professor at Rutgers University in New Jersey and contain articles by numerous Black scholars all making significant contributions to the study of ancient Blacks. C.A. Diop's, *THE AFRICAN ORIGIN OF CIVILIZATION* is probably the single most helpful secular source on ancient Blacks. He brings the perspectives of a critical scholar and a native African to the subject and documents the Negroid identity of many biblical countries.

In 1925, the Reverend R.A. Morrisey wrote in his book, *COL-ORED PEOPLE AND BIBLE HISTORY:*

> Every foremost race of people in the world today has its history written by its own members. To keep this universal rule, colored people should be no exception...because the information as well as inspiration will lead their own group toward nobler aspirations and higher ideals in life's activities ...The Negro has a history of which he need not be ashamed, but he will wait a long time for a White man to write this history in fairness, for the consumption of the great White public. [29]

Morrisey is right. If Black Biblical history is going to be written it must be written by a Black man because as this study reveals, it is highly unlikely that White writers will fairly address our Biblical history. Therefore, we pay tribute to all Black men and women who have labored to make contributions toward this essential field of study. Furthermore, we salute churches who have made the study of Blacks in the Bible a part of their church school curriculum or annually devote a Sunday or several days to study in honor of our glorious past.

NOTES
CHAPTER 4

1. Dr. Anthony T. Evans, Are Blacks Spiritually Inferior To Whites?, Renaissance Productions, Inc., Wenonah, NJ, 1992, pp. 32-33.

2. Walter Arthur McCray, The Black Presence in the Bible, Black Light Fellowship, Chicago, IL, 1990, p.31.

3. Dr. Carter Woodson, "Quotelines," USA Today, February 1, 1989, p. 8A.

4. Anthony T. Browder, From the Browder File: 22 Essays on the African American Experience, The Institute of Karmic Guidance, Washington, D.C., 1989, 1p. 19.

5. Dr. E.V. Hill, "And God Made Man," Genesis 1:27, Sermon on Tape, Concord Missionary Baptist Church, 3410 S. Polk, Dallas, TX, August 15, 1985.

6. Chuck Singleton, "The Biblical Response to Malcolm X," Genesis 9:24-29, 10:1-20, Sermon on Tape, Loveland Church, 16888 Baseline Ave., Fontana, CA, 92335, December 6, 1992.

7. Adam Clayton Powell, Jr., Adam by Adam: The Autobiography of Adam Clayton Powell, Jr., The Dial Press, New York, 1971, pp. 243-244.

8. Cain Hope Felder, Troubling Biblical Waters: Race, Class, and Family, Orbis Books, Maryknoll, NY, 1989, Information regarding the conversion of Black Muslim inmates was communicated in a telephone conversation with Dr. Felder in Oct. 1993.

9. Judy Howard, "Bible's Black Tradition Ignored, Author Says," The Dallas Morning News, February 24, 1990, Metropolitan Section. For additional information, also see Eddie Lane, Book Reviews, Bibliotheca Sacra, April-June 1990, pp. 244-245.

10. Dr. Manuel L. Scott, Sr., "The Church in Christ's Perspective, Mark 11:17," 86th Annual Session, National Baptist Congress of Christian Education, Unpublished Booklet, June 18-21, 1991.

11. Kenneth C. Ulmer, "Black History In the Bible," Sermon on Tape, Faithful Central Baptist Church, Los Angeles, February 19, 1984.

12. David Adamo, The Place of Africa and Africans in the Old Testament and Its Environment, UMI Dissertation Information Service, 1986, Ann Arbor, MI, p. IV.

13. Ibid., p.V.

14. Charles B. Copher, Stoney the Road We Trod: African American Biblical Interpretation, Fortress Press, Minneapolis, 1991, pp. 146-164, edited by Cain Hope Felder.

15. Charles B. Copher, Black Biblical Studies: An Anthology of Charles B. Copher, Biblical and Theological Issues on the Black Presence in the Bible, Black Light Fellowship, Chicago, IL, 1993, p. 116.

16. Ibid., p. V.118

17. Walter Arthur McCray, The Black Presence in the Bible and the Table of Nations, Genesis 10:1-32: With Emphasis on the Hamitic Genealogical Line from a Black Perspective, Black Light Fellowship, Chicago, IL, 1990, Vol. II, p. 73.

18. Holy Bible, King James Version, Original African Heritage Edition, The James C. Winston Publishing Company, Nashville, TN, 1993, p. ix.

19. C.L. Franklin, Give Me This Mountain, edited by Jeff Todd Titon, University of Illinois Press, 1989, p. 187.

20. Renita J. Weems, Just A Sister Away: A Womanist Vision of Women's Relationships in the Bible, Lura Media, San Diego, CA, 1988, p. 1.

21. Perryman, "The Curse of Ham," Sermon on Tape, Friendship Baptist Church, 17145 Bast Anchury Rd., Yorba Linda, CA, 92686, July 26, 1993, James D. Carrington, Pastor.

22. Ibid.

23. Ibid.

24. W.E. Burghardt DuBois, The Negro, Oxford University Press, Inc., London, Oxford, New York, 1970, p. 11.

25. Ibid.

26. Bishop Alfred G. Dunston, Jr., The Black Man in the Old Testament and Its World, Africa World Press, Inc., Trenton, NJ, 1992, p. X.

27. Ernest C. Sargent, III, Majestic Honor: Biblical Perspectives In Black History, Charity Church, Fort Worth, TX, 1992, p. 10.

28. Alvin A. Jones, Royalty Without A Future, Christian Faith Ministries, P.O. Box 90824, Washington, D.C., 20090, 1992, p. 17.

29. R. A. Morrisey, Colored People and Bible History, W. B. Conkey, Hammond, Indiana, 1925, Quoted by Cain Hope Felder, Troubling Biblical Waters: Race, Class, and Family, p. xii.

Chapter 5

REFUTING THE 'GOOD OLD BOY' PERSPECTIVE

Blacks cannot rely solely on White scholars to teach us our origin, history, and contributions to civilization prior to slavery in America. If we rely on White scholars we would conclude that our appearance on the scene of world history came about by a drunken man, by the mark of Cain (Gen. 4:15), by the theory of evolution, or by coincidental environmental factors. Furthermore, we would conclude our dark skin was due to thousands of years in the sun. And being like "Johnny Come Latelys" we never made significant contributions to ancient history except through the Ethiopians and many would debate their classification as Negroid or Black.

All of the aforementioned arguments of the Black Man's origin are totally unacceptable. As a matter of fact, it would take more faith to believe those theories than the simple truth and the reliable historical facts of God's Word. The purpose of this chapter is to respond to the arguments, present our convictions in support of the Black presence in Scripture, and finally respond to the curse of the Ham theory.

1. Theological and respected secular testimonies regarding Blacks have probably been the most important factor that led to the erroneous conclusion that Blacks made no valuable contributions to the Biblical world. The six following views exemplify the thinking of those who refuse to accept Black presence and significance in the Scripture.

A. THE INTERNATIONAL STANDARD BIBLE ENCYCLOPEDIA (1956 edition) states under the section entitled Ham:

> Of the nationalities regarded as descended from Ham, none can be described as really Black. First on the list, as being the darkest is Cush or Ethiopia (Gen. 10:6). ...it is noteworthy that some of them, like the Ethiopians and the Canaanites, spoke Semitic, and not Hamitic languages. [1]

To most Black Americans the ISBE's definition of Ham is seen as a fallacy, for the Ethiopians are classified as a Black race.

B. William F. Albright a renown scholar in the field of biblical archaeology stated in THE INTERPRETERS BIBLE,

All known ancient races in the region which concerns us here [biblical world] belonged to the so-called 'White' or 'Caucasian' race... [2]

Albright does believe that the Cushites and Nubians were Negroid. Nevertheless, the bold statement quoted above paints a picture in the average mind that the biblical world was "lily white."

C. THE PICTORIAL BIBLE DICTIONARY under its Ham entry states, He became progenitor of the dark races; not the Negroes,... [3]

Even when there is mention of "dark races" they are classified as something other than Negroes.

D. David Hume, a respected philosopher who wrote in the latter half of the eighteenth century, stated:

I am apt to suspect the Negroes, and in general all the other species of men (for there are four or five different kinds) to be naturally inferior to the Whites. There never was a civilized nation of any other complexion than White, nor even any individual eminent either in action or speculation. No ingenious manufactures amongst them, no arts, no sciences...

In Jamaica indeed they talk of one Negro as a man of parts and learning; but for this he is likely admired for a very slender accomplishment, like a parrot, who speaks a few words plainly. [4]

E. The historian, Arnold Toynbee wrote:

It will be seen that, when we classify mankind by color, the only primary race that has not made a creative contribution to any civilization is the Black race. [5]

Far and wide, the popular view during the Renaissance period and in modern history is that Blacks are an inferior race. The same view is reflective in the beliefs held today by the majority of White America, Europeans, Christians and non-Christians. Unfortunately, the thinking represented above is pervasive in our society.

F. Even a former President, admired to this day by our current President, had this to say about the intellectual capacities of Blacks. Thomas Jefferson in his Notes on Virginia wrote:

Comparing them by their faculties of memory, reason, and imagination, it appears to me, that in memory they are equal to the Whites; in reason much inferior...and that in imagination they are dull, tasteless and anomalous...never yet could I find that a Black had uttered a thought above the level of plain narration; never see even an elementary trait of painting or sculpture. [6]

The opinions of opinion-makers have contributed to the belief that there were no Blacks in the Bible and that they made no significant contributions to history. We believe that the thinking of most Whites, even those who do not profess to be prejudice, will reflect Hume's belief that, "There never was a civilized nation of any other complexion than White."[7] As a matter of fact, the American public school system as well as White Theological Academic institutions in essence teach Hume's viewpoint on civilized nations. They fail to teach about the advanced civilizations in central Africa, or even inner Africa's influence on the development of Egypt. To perpetuate their White superiority viewpoint, they classify the Egyptians and all the Nile Valley civilizations as White even though these nations are among the nations of Ham listed in Genesis Ten. It is this thinking that prevents us from making meaningful impact in resolving our race problems.

2. The second argument denying the full biblical heritage of Blacks is the TOWER OF BABEL AND THE ENVIRONMENT THEORY. This theory is the most commonly accepted viewpoint on the origin of races. As a matter of fact, we believed it until we researched Genesis 9:18-29 and Genesis Ten. What is the Tower of Babel and the Environment theory?

C.L. Franklin adequately summarized the environment view on the origin of the races when he preached from the text of Genesis 9:20-29. Franklin preached this message at the New Bethel Baptist Church in Detroit Michigan where he pastored:

The part of the world from which you came is responsible for your color. You [addressing Blacks] lived in a tropical situation originally, where the sun was severe, and generations of heat effectuated the color that you are now. If you have a broad nose, it is because nature did that, in order that your intake of oxygen would be great enough for you to survive; because in the kind of intense heat that you came from, out of that part of the world from which you came, with a thin, closed-up nose, you couldn't have lived. Your oxygen intake would not have been sufficient for survival. [8]

Franklin did not mention the Tower of Babel in his message. But the standard argument is that people on the face of the earth lived together and traveled as a unit up until the Tower of Babel recorded in Genesis 11:1-9. It is believed that when the people spread across the face of the earth, those who migrated to the North (Europe) became of a light complexion after a period of time; those who moved to the south (Africa and all southern locations below the Equator) became dark over a period of time; and those who lived in Asia became medium or brown. According to the Bible, there were no language differences until after the Tower of Babel (Gen. 11:1,7,8). Consequently, it is assumed that racial distinctions did not come into existence until the scattering at the Tower of Babel.

According to Frank Snowden in his book BEFORE COLOR PREJUDICE, "...the Greeks perhaps by the sixth century B.C. had begun to seek an explanation of the physical differences between the extremely fair and the very dark."[9] Snowden made the following noteworthy comments amplifying this subject in a sub section classified "The Environment Theory of Racial Differences":

> The view that...human inhabitants of a region and their manner of life are determined to a large extent by diversity of climatic, topographical, and hydrographical conditions first appears in the Hippocratic Corpus. According to Pliny, heat is responsible for the scorched complexion, curly beards and hair, and tall stature of the Ethiopians, and the mobility of climate explains their wisdom; moisture in the opposite region of the world accounts for the tall men of the north with their white frosty skin and straight, yellow hair, their White fierceness resulting from rigidity of the climate; a mix of fire and moisture in the middle region of the earth explains men of medium stature, with a blended complexion and with gentle customs and fertile intellects. [10]

Snowden quoted Arnold Toynbee who said, the Greeks explained obvious physical differences "as being the effects of diverse environments upon a uniform human nature, instead of seeing in them the outward manifestations of a diversity that was somewhat intrinsic in human nature itself." [11] Toynbee raised an alternative viewpoint that is "intrinsic in human nature." We call Toynbee's viewpoint the genetic, biblical viewpoint which is a more plausible explanation for the origin of the races of mankind. We have three primary objections to the Tower of Babel and the Environment view concerning the origin of the races of mankind.

First, the Tower of Babel and the Environment viewpoint is based on the premise that the complexion of people on the face of the earth was fair prior to the scattering at the Tower of Babel. There is no historical or scientific basis for this assumption. In fact, the evidence is quite the contrary. [12] However, this theory is so popular and prevalent that a seminary professor said to a friend, "There is no evidence of any Black person in the Bible prior to the assembly at the Tower of Babel." [13] And of course, if Blacks came into the Scripture after the Tower of Babel, it is difficult to determine in Scripture who was Black.

This theory gives Whites a clear and certain foundation in Scripture and in ancient history. This theory leaves people of color, specifically Blacks, with a confused, cluttered and uncertain foundation. According to this theory, Whites know their origin but for Blacks and people of color, origin remains a mystery. Consequently, the question is often raised, where did Blacks originate? However, with an objective study of ancient history, the question is easily eliminated with many answers, even the question "Where did Whites originate?"

We must look beyond the claims of the Greeks and find sensible, scriptural answers from the book of Genesis. In so doing, one race will not be given a historical advantage over the other.

Genesis 11: 7,8 makes it clear that diversity of languages and global population distribution took place after the attempt to build the Tower of Babel. But no mention is made of the development of races after the Tower of Babel because we believe that racial distinctions were already in place at the Tower of Babel. Genesis Ten seeks to explain racial origins and developments. We are aware of the chronological order of Genesis Eleven occurring before the account of Genesis Ten. We are also aware that the people at the Tower of Babel were also present in Genesis Ten (i.e. Nimrod, Genesis 10:8-12).

Our second objection to the Tower of Babel and the Environment theory is that it implies that Blacks became black accidentally or unintentionally. This theory suggests that God intended for man to be White and it was by the sun man became dark. This theory also suggests that God favors Whites, for after all, He made them first and the other races came into existence coincidentally. This theory contradicts the Scripture: "Hath not one God created all equal" (Malachi 2:10) and "God is no respecter of persons" (Acts 10:34). If God made Whites, and they were the only people in the world prior to the Tower of Babel, this would mean that God respected them above others. It would mean that God gave them unfair advantage and place in history.

This theory gives Whites almost an exclusive claim to the full content of the Bible. Hence, contributing to a feeling of superiority toward Blacks resulting in prejudice and racism. They are aided by the church, the media, and school systems. The end result for Blacks is a mind full of soul searching questions: Where did we originate? Why did God curse our race and allow us to be used in history as tools for the Europeans? Why aré we not included in God's Holy Bible? And the questions multiply.

The Tower of Babel theory is objectionable because it ultimately suggests that Blacks are "Johnny Come Latelys," on the scene of world history. We were not conceived in the mind of God during creation as the White race, but progressed into blackness. The theory continues to suggest that we never developed into a great nation and when Blacks excel or succeed, such progress is not the rule, but the exception to the rule. As far as we are concerned, the Tower of Babel theory is just as bad as the curse of Ham theory, because they are both based on the viewpoint that it is inferior to be Black.

One reason we believe many in White academia, both consciously and subconsciously promulgate the Tower of Babel theory, and speculate on other views regarding the Black man's complexion, is to protect their lofty status.

Our third and final objection to the Tower of Babel and the Environment theory is that on several counts it contradicts Scripture. Acts 17:26, states that "God hath taken one blood and made all nations of men", and again God has taken "one blood" and not "one blood and one sun". Therefore, we refuse to believe or teach that nations or races were produced by one sun--unless "sun" is spelled--"Son." "All things were made by Him; and without Him was not anything made that was made" (John 1:3). Since God made man, all mankind (red, yellow, black, and white) came from the loins of Adam; and the sun or the environment did not produce the complexion of man in the Garden. And God made man in His image and in His likeness (Gen. 1:26).

We agree with St. Augustine who wrote:

What is true for a Christian beyond the shadow of a doubt is that every real man, that is, every mortal animal that is rational, however, unusual to us may be the shape of his body, or the color of his skin, or the way he walks, or the sound of his voice, and whatever the strength, portion or quality of his natural endowments, is descended from the single first-created man. [14]

In another passage Augustine writes,

...the whole human race, which was to become Adam's posterity through the first woman, was present in the first man. [15]

Neither Augustine in his book, THE CITY OF GOD, nor Josephus in his book ANTIQUITIES OF THE JEWS, used the Tower of Babel to originate the theory of racial diversity. [16] We realize that this is an argument from silence, nevertheless, our point is the Tower of Babel theory is not in Scripture.

We therefore conclude that the Tower of Babel and the Environment theory only serves the false notion of White Superiority from the beginning of time until today. The Tower of Babel theory is racist to the core. Although racism may or may not have been the motivation behind those who developed the theory, when it is critically analyzed, it falls short of sound doctrine and supports racism. Unfortunately, because Blacks have not critically thought through this issue, we ignorantly carry the same viewpoints of the theorists.

For those who ascribe to the Tower of Babel and the Environment view, the fact of a Black presence in Scripture and their greatness in ancient history would be considered fiction, romanticism or flatly lies.

In recent years, we are beginning to see White scholars voice alternative views regarding the origin of the races. This was evident in the January 11, 1988 issue of Newsweek which featured a Black Adam and Eve on its front cover. The article suggested that all mankind who descended from Eve, an African, should be known as Eve.[17] We believe the Tower of Babel theory will continue to be "debunked" because the universe was built on truth. Hence, we believe that in these last days God is raising up men and women, White and Black, liberal and conservative who speak the truth regarding the Black presence in Scripture and in ancient history.

3. Another argument against the Black presence in Scripture and the prominence of Blacks in ancient history is the defining of race. Can we apply twentieth century definitions of race to early history? Are there universal definitions of race from which we can define race in this discussion?

There is a morass of confusion in defining race, especially in deciphering race origins in ancient history and the biblical world. The disarrangement is due to the lack of a universal acceptance of definitions for the essence of race. There also exists a lack of knowledge regarding the tenth chapter of Genesis--the Table of Nations and the issue of racial origins.

Admittedly, the one who coins the definition of a given race controls the argument concerning the Black race. It is obvious, therefore, that Blacks have been categorically excluded from Scripture since Whites have controlled the definition. They have controlled the printing presses, public school system and the public media from the inception of America. Even though Blacks were freed from slavery in 1863, many of us were never freed from the chains around our minds.

One reason that many in the African-American community reject the issue of biblical ethnicity is due to a chained mind. Our minds are burdened with the weight of White academia's definition of race, and we, by default, have allowed them to dictate our origin and destiny.

This was illustrated in the movie "Malcolm X", Malcolm expressed an interest in becoming a lawyer in elementary school. He was subjected to the tightening of the chain of oppression when his White male teacher told him he was better suited to become a carpenter.

Since Blacks have not been the ones to develop the definitions and classifications of race, we have allowed academia to develop the definitions for Caucasians. These definitions are not only contradictory, but confusing. Our mere nonchalance has literally allowed others to commit academic armed robbery against our history. Consequently, due to academia's success at chaining our minds, it took a Dallas pastor about fifteen minutes to convince another pastor that Egypt was a part of Africa. In his mind Egypt was located in southern Europe or the Middle East. He was shocked to discover that Egypt was in Africa - which underscores the fact that western academia had been successful in putting chains around our mind.

The first thing Blacks are taught about themselves in school is that we are descendants of slaves, who arrived in America from the west coast of Africa. In contrast, our children are taught that Whites were the creators of western civilizations: Greece, Rome, France, England, and America. Our children, Black and White, are taught that western civilizations produced the first physician of antiquity - Hippocrates; the father of history - Herodotus; great philosophers - Socrates and Plato; and the great scientists - Galileo and Sir Isaac Newton. Rarely are Black or White children taught about the great nations of North, East and Central Africa; and if so, they are never taught that all of Africa, including Egypt and Ethiopia, was initially occupied and dominated by Blacks. Academia never broadcast the name Imhotep - a distinguished physician in Egyptian history who practiced medicine before Greece became a nation. Academia never recognized Manatheo - who wrote the history of Egypt before Herodotus was born. Queen Ti - who once ruled Egypt and whose statues leave no doubt that she was Black.

Western Education has successfully placed chains on our minds. White children leave history classes knowing countries and names of White heroes and heroines who have made great contributions to the history of mankind. While at the other hand, Black children leave the history class without acknowledging Africa, a great country with rich ethnic history and many great heros and heroines. We have allowed chains to be placed around our minds.

Blacks were never taught the great accomplishments of Africans in the Western and Eurocentric school systems. They were not taught that the ancient Ethiopians, Egyptians, Nubians and other descendants of Ham, (Africa was once known as The Land of Ham), produced clocks and calendars, maps and gears, architecture, engineering, medicine and mathematics. Africans were the ones who first named and map the stars, were the first to practice religion and taught students from Greece on African soil. We were never taught that Greek civilization was a copy of Egyptian and Ethiopian civilizations. WE HAVE ALLOWED CHAINS TO BE PLACED AROUND OUR MINDS.

CAN WE BREAK THE CHAINS AROUND OUR MINDS? We believe we Can! Jesus said, "And ye shall know the truth and the truth shall set you free" (John 8:32). Precisely, the only way to break the chains around our minds is to know the truth. We have not been told the truth about our racial origin and heritage, therefore, we should not leave it to others to tell us who we are, but we must labor to answer those questions for ourselves.

As we study this matter of ancient ethnicity, we can see the magnitude of the disaster against the Black race in ancient and modern history. The media has been solely responsible for our demise. However, we have good news. THE CHAINS CAN BE BROKEN! THE CHAINS WILL BE BROKEN! THE CHAINS ARE BEING BROKEN! WHAT WILL BREAK THE CHAINS? THE TRUTH! WHAT IS THE TRUTH? Jesus said, 'Sanctify them in the truth; Thy Word is truth' (John 17:17). Whose responsibility is it to communicate this truth? THE CHURCH'S. God has commissioned the church to preach the truth. The truth includes the origins and development of the races of mankind. We are absolutely convinced that many of the social problems plaguing the Black community today is due to the vast majority of Blacks who have never heard the truth regarding our racial origins and development.

(1) The popular definition of Caucasian are people who are generally considered to be people of the fairest and lightest complexions in the world. To the average American, White is indicative of a descendant of Europe who typically may have straight hair ranging from blond to black in color. Their eye color is usually blue, brown, black or green; and they typically speak an Indo-European language. As a matter of fact, the color adjective ascribed to Caucasians--"White"--indicates lightest of all colors. In the popular understanding of the word "Caucasian," light-skinned Latinos, and the slightly dark southern Italians and Greeks are said to be members of the Caucasian family, in spite of the fact that they are darker than the typical White Caucasian. In addition, the media always project Bible characters who reflect the popular definition of Caucasian.

The popular definition of Caucasian is reflected in encyclopedias, although, they reveal hints of a wider, more inclusive, definition. We know that there will be little disagreement with the above definition of Caucasian. Wherever the word Caucasian is read, be it in history, anthropology, or theology or any other book or magazine, the images that comes to mind are the ones described above. THE WEBSTER'S STUDENT DICTIONARY defines Caucasian:

1. Of or relating to the Caucasus or its inhabitants.
2. Of or belonging to the native languages of the Caucasus region.
3. Of or belonging to the division of mankind comprising the chief races of Europe, North Africa, and south western Asia, named the Caucasian race in the belief [18] that the people of the Caucasus were typical of the race.

THE NEW LEXICON WEBSTER'S DICTIONARY OF THE ENGLISH LANGUAGE gives this definition,

1. n. a person of the Caucasus; the family of languages spoken there; a member of the predominately white-skinned race (after a skull found in the Caucasus) one of the three main divisions of mankind, living generally in Europe, western Asia and North Africa. (cf. Mongolian, cf. Negro)

2. adj. pertaining to the region of Caucasia, its inhabitants, or the languages native to it; of or pertaining to the White race of mankind. [19]

The NEW LEXICON WEBSTER'S DICTIONARY OF THE ENGLISH LANGUAGE gives the following definitions for "Caucasia" and "Caucasoid":

1. Caucasia...(or Caucasus) the region of the southwest U.S.S.R. between the Black Sea and the Caspian crossed by the Caucasus. It was formerly divided into Cisaucasia...north of the mountains, considered as being Europe, and Transcaucasia, south of them considered as a part of Asia (now Georgia, Armenia, and Azerbaijan).

Caucasoid...1. adj. of or pertaining to the Caucasian race

2. n. a member of the Caucasian race. [20]

From the above four definitions we learn several things about Caucasians pertinent to our subject matter.

(1) Caucasians are one of "the three main divisions of mankind." The "MONGOLIAN" and "NEGRO" according to THE NEW LEXICON WEBSTER'S DICTIONARY are defined as Caucasian. Mongoloids and Negroes are definitely not considered Caucasians. (However, we will discover that the anthropological and technical

definitions of Caucasian describes features identical to most Black people).

(2) Caucasians generally live in "Europe, North Africa, and south-western Asia." This definition places "Caucasians" on three major continents - Europe, Asia and Africa. Thus, academia is afforded the license to label any person or nation on those continents as Caucasian. The biblical and ancient lands comprise southern Europe, North Africa, and southwestern Asia.

(3) Twice in the above definitions are Caucasians referred to as "white-skinned" or "white race."

(4) The word "Caucasian" is a derivative of the once geographic location in what was the U.S.S.R. called "Caucasia." Caucasia was located in southern Europe bordering southwest Asia.

(5) The Caucasian race was named in the belief that the people of the Caucasus were typical of the race. The Caucasus according to the NEW WEBSTER'S LEXICON DICTIONARY was a "mountain system of the U.S.S.R. ...that runs diagonally across the land bridge between the Black Sea and the Caspian as a solid wall...along the Iranian border." [21] It would be a plausible assumption that the people of the Caucasus mountains or Caucasia were a "white-skinned" people since they were typical of the Caucasian race.

(6) The Caucasians living in North Africa, southwestern Asia and Europe are implied to have no substantial difference one from the other. Caucasians outside of the Caucasus mountain area in other parts of Europe, Asia, and Africa, were very similar to the Caucasians of Caucasia-"white-skinned", even with a slight variation in color.

(7) It would appear that the original home of the Caucasians, based on the above definitions, would be Europe; since that is where Cauca-sians are predominately located.

Again, the above definition for Caucasians places Caucasians in North Africa, Asia and Europe. THE NEW LEXICON WEBSTER'S DICTIONARY, however, the definition for "Negro" does not place Negroes in Africa, Asia or Europe.

Negro - n. a member of the dark skinned race, one of the three major divisions of the races of mankind, living in Africa south of the Sahara. [22]

Refuting The 'Good Old Boy' Perspective 85

Descriptions of Caucasians at least from the popular use of the term, would not be said to come from North Africa or southwestern Asia; because the dominant groups in North Africa and southwestern Asia (particularly in antiquity) do not match the typical descriptions and features of Caucasians. Knowing migration patterns, we do believe that there were "typical" Caucasians in North Africa and southwestern Asia. However, we also believe that Caucasians were decisively in the minority until the invasion of southwestern Asia and North Africa by the Greeks in 330 B.C. Herodotus, who was an eyewitness in Egypt near 500 B.C. certainly did not describe the North African Egyptians as "white-skinned." He described them as "black-skinned."

According to *The New Lexicon Websters Dictionary* (NLWD), Negroes are restricted to sub-Sahara Africa, and with the stroke of a pen, Caucasians are given North Africa and Southwestern Asia. The NLWD dictionary clearly establishes Caucasians in Europe, Asia, and North Africa - which are biblical lands - the cradle of civilization; and limits Negroes to sub-Saharan Africa. This our friends, is tantamount to "academic rape" pertaining to the Black or Negro race of mankind. But the definitions become even clear.

WEBSTER'S THIRD NEW INTERNATIONAL DICTIONARY gives the following definitions for "Hamite", "Japhetic" and "Semite":

Hamite

1: a descendant of Ham, one of the sons of Noah

2a: a member of a group of African peoples including the Berber peoples north of the Sahara, the Tauregs and Tibbu in the Judan, possibly the extinct Guanches of the Canaries, the ancient Egyptians and their descendants, and the Galla of East Africa that are mostly Muslims, are highly variable in appearance but mainly Caucasoid, and are believed by many to be late - Paleolithic or post -Paleolithic colonists of western Europe.

2b: a native speaker of a Hamitic language - compare Copt. Ethiopian.[23]

Japhetic

1: relating to or derived from Japheth who was a son of Noah - used vaguely as an ethnological epithet for the Caucasians of Europe and some adjacent parts of Asia. [24]

Semite

1: a member of one of the peoples listed in the Scriptures as descended from Shem, a son of Noah.

2: a member of one of the group of peoples of southwestern Asia
speaking Semitic languages and chiefly represented now by Jews and
Arabs but in ancient time by Babylonians, Assyrians, Arameans,
Canaanites and Phonecians. [25]

In regard to the above definitions, Noah's son Japheth is clearly
associated with Europe, "Caucasians" and some adjacent parts of Asia."
Noah's son Shem, is clearly associated with southwestern Asia and some of
the better known countries and people of the biblical world. (Although
Semitic persons reflect a wide range of complexions, academia still classifies them as Caucasians.) Noah's son Ham is associated with "African
peoples...highly variable in appearance but mainly Caucasoid."
    Once again Africans located in the biblical world are labeled
"Caucasoid." Japheth and Shem "walked" off the pages into the mind of
the reader appearing Caucasian - European or Semitic. Ham also
"walked" off the page appearing as if he was a "Caucasoid." Remember
Caucasoid means "of or pertaining to the Caucasian race - a member of the
Caucasian race." Specifically, Ham's descendants were "highly variable in
appearance" (whatever that means) but mainly Caucasoid. (Is the phrase
"highly variable in appearance" a subtle admission that the Hamites were a
dark complexioned people?)
    According to the above definitions, the Japhetic, Semitic and
Hamitic people are all Caucasians, thus meaning there are no Negroids
among Noah's descendants. Because White people were writing the
dictionaries, all of Noah's descendants are classified Caucasians.

The unedited entry of "HAMITE" in the FUNK AND WAGNALLS
NEW ENCYCLOPEDIA, stated:

HAMITE, group of Caucasian people, originally of northern and
northeastern Africa and the Canary Islands. Anthropologist are in
dispute about the precise ethnological definition of the Hamite; they
generally define the group as including the following: the Berber of
North Africa; the Fula, Tuareg, and Tibbu of the Sudan; the ancient
Egyptians; the major Ethiopian peoples; and the Guanche, an extinct
people of the Canary Islands.

The typical Hamite is relatively tall and has dark brown skin and curly
black hair. Some ethnologist have attempted to link the Hamite with
the Mediterranean peoples, thus tracing their origin to Europe.

The Hamites are in the main agricultural peoples. They are credited with originating the oldest extant writing in the world, the hiero-glyphic inscriptions of the ancient Egyptians, and were the earliest engineers and architects to work in Massive stone.[26]

When we read the above encyclopedic explanation of Hamite we were absolutely startled. We stood in amazement at the length to which Western and Eurocentric academia will go to in order to deny Blacks a biblical heritage. It is quite obvious to Blacks and Whites in America that "dark-brown skin and curly black hair" people from the African continent hardly deserves the appellation - "Caucasian peoples." The FUNK AND WAGNALL'S Hamite entry provides a good laugh for most Blacks because not just brown, but "dark brown skin" and not just black hair, but "curly black hair" simply does not describe a Caucasian in the world.

Funk and Wagnalls', THE GROLIER ENCYCLOPEDIA, and every European scholar who labels the Hamites "Caucasian", we believe fully understand that they are utilizing a technical, academic definition for racial classifications which remove color as a criteria for determining race. John Q Citizen is unaware, because it is never explained, that the academic and technical definition of Caucasian is significantly different from the popular definition of Caucasian. GROLIER ENCYCLOPEDIA reveals an anthropological technical definition of "Caucasoid" that includes the following descriptions - "dark brown," "wavy," "curliness," "wooly," and "frizzy" hair. [27] These descriptions would allow practically all people of color around the world to be classified as Caucasians. GROLIER explains this technical/academic definition of Caucasoid:

> Caucasoid - one of the major groups of mankind, skin color varies from White to dark brown. ...The Caucasoid major group... includes...many peoples of dark skin color, such as the Australian Aborigines...Mediterranean, Hamitic...and Polynesian. [28]

By labeling all of the above as "Caucasoid", Blacks are being denied a place in the Biblical World [Hamitic]. This represents an aca-demic sleight of hand interchanging a popular definition with a technical definition without explanation. This our friends is WRONG! WRONG! WRONG! The method of application denies Blacks a heritage in biblical and ancient history. Any Australian Aborigine walking the street of America would be labeled "Caucasoid" - which is known as "a member of the Caucasian race." Since Eurocentric academia labels the Aborigine and Hamites "Caucasoid" or "dark brown", persons with "wooly" or "curly" hair as Caucasoid; then they need to label the vast majority of American Negroes as Caucasoid. They will then have to apologize for slavery and segregation in America based on skin color. The broad, contradictory, inconsistent, "self serving," and hypocritical European definitions of "Caucasians" have allowed White scholars to "honestly" state that there were no Blacks in the Bible. We believe that dictionaries, encyclopedias, and text books that have not and will not tell the truth print about ancient ethnicity, inflicting as much harm on Blacks as the Ku Klux Klan. Curiously scholarly opinions, the Tower of Babel theory, and devious usages of definitions, have all worked together to deny Blacks a history worthy of a chronicle.

4. The fourth and final argument against a significant Black presence in Scripture concerns the curse of the Black man in Scripture. His name is Ham. What is the "curse of Ham theory"?

This theory is based on the Genesis 9:18-29 which states that God and Noah pronounced a life long curse on Ham and his descendants. The curse was for reasons ranging from sexual impropriety with Noah or his wife, to simply seeing the nakedness of his father. Furthermore, the curse pronounced upon Ham caused he and his descendants to become dark skinned; to have thick lips, a big nose, kinky hair; and to forever be assigned to servantry to the descendants of Japheth and Shem.

The curse of Ham theory is held by a great number of people in our day and time. A Black preacher was asked by a White colleague of ours, what was the nature of his recent sermons. The Black preacher responded, "Blacks In The Bible." Our White colleague, a Master of Divinity Seminary graduate and pastor of one of the largest churches in Fort Worth, said, "I wouldn't do that because Blacks come from the curse of Ham."

Dr. R.E. Fowler of Fort Worth, the Black preacher, lectured on the Black Presence in Scripture at Texas Christian University in February 1993. During the Q and A session, a White professor stood up and said, he could prove from the Bible that Ham was cursed. Dr. Fowler said, "Okay prove it, let's read the text." As the White professor read Genesis 9: 18-29, he discovered it was not Ham who was cursed but Canaan, Ham's youngest son. The professor then responded, "I've been wrong all this time." Two White men with advanced academic degrees, who had simply accepted a teaching handed down to them, that has denigrated an entire race of people. They did not take the time to critically investigate the issue. We could cite many examples, but the point has been sufficiently addressed.

The "curse of Ham", is still a widely held view because it has been taught by well respected White scholars throughout history. C.I. Scofield author of the renown Scofield Reference Bible made the following comments on Genesis 9:24-27. (Scofield's Bible was first copyrighted in 1909 and published by Oxford University Press.)

> A prophetic declaration is made that from Ham will descend an inferior and servile posterity (Gen. 9:24,25).
>
> A prophetic declaration is made that Shem will have a peculiar relation to Jehovah (Gen. 9:26,27). All divine relation is through Semitic men, and Christ, after the flesh, descends from Shem.
>
> A prophetic declaration is made that from Japheth will descend the "enlarged" races (Gen. 9:27). Government, science, and art, speaking broadly, are and have been Japhetic, so that history is the indisputable record of the exact fulfillment of these declarations. [29]

Although Scofield makes no direct references to Caucasian or Negroid races in his comments, it is clearly understood in the minds of his readers that Ham represents the Blacks and Shem and Japheth represents Whites. A study of Genesis 9:18-29 could leave an objective reader with the conclusion that Ham's descendants would be inferior and "servile posterity."

The SMITH'S BIBLE DICTIONARY published by Holman Bible Publishers of Nashville, Tenn. in 1991, in a section entitled "Four Thousand Questions and Answers", answers two questions related to the curse of Ham:

> Which of Noah's sons brought a curse on his posterity by his conduct to his father or this occasion? --Ham.
>
> Do the effects of this curse continue to the present time? Where? Yes: in Africa, which was peopled by descendants of Ham, and is the chief scene of the horrible traffic in slaves. [30]

The curse of Ham theory places Blacks in the Bible but as an "inferior", "servile", and "cursed" people. If the race of Blacks were cursed by God or Noah at the dawn of history, then they could not have played a prominent role in history or in the Bible.

We want to offer several responses to the curse of Ham theory: First, it was Canaan who was cursed, not Ham (Gen. 9:25). Secondly, Ham was a 100 years old by the time of the curse, he already had a color identity (Gen. 5:32). Thirdly, we are in agreement with Josephus, Custance, and Peterson who explained why Canaan was cursed and not Ham.

Josephus said, regarding the "curse of Ham,"

> ...but for Ham, he [Noah] did not curse him, by reason of his nearness in blood, but cursed his posterity. [31]

Arthur C. Custance, taking a flight off Josephus' runway, argued:

> What is important to note is that Noah could not pronounce judgment of any kind upon his son, Ham, the actual offender, without passing judgement upon himself, for society held him, the father responsible for his son's behavior. To punish Ham, then, he must of necessity pronounce a curse upon Canaan, Ham's son. [32]

Carlisle John Peterson, a Black Canadian writer, provides an interesting interpretation of this incident in his book THE DESTINY OF THE BLACK RACE:

> Concerning the cursing of Ham..., Ham was not cursed but his son Canaan was. Why was this? We must understand that when the son of man in covenant with God violates his covenantal duty, that son does not experience the consequence of his transgression in his lifetime but his son experiences the consequences of his father's violation of the covenant. This is not done for the sake of the person who violates the covenant but for the [name] sake of God's covenant to His covenant - man. When Solomon violated his covenantal duty towards God, the Kingdom was not taken from him but it was taken from his son.
>
> 1 Kings 11:11-13 states as follows:
>
> v.11 Therefore the Lord said to Solomon, Because you have done this, and have not kept My covenant and My statutes, which I have commanded you, I will surely tear the kingdom away from you and give it to your servant.
>
> v.12 Nevertheless, I will not do it in your days, for the sake of your father David; I will tear it out of the hand of your son.
>
> v.13 However, I will not tear away the whole kingdom; I will give one tribe to your son for the sake of my servant David, and for the sake of Jerusalem which I have chosen.

As we see from this passage, the reason Solomon was not punished was for the sake of the covenant God made with David. In the same way, the reason Ham was not cursed was for the sake of the covenant that God made with Noah, so that Noah would not be defamed. Thus, Ham's son was cursed, just as Solomon's son Rehoboam was cursed, because of their father's violation of the covenant. So Noah passed the curse on to Canaan to punish him convenantally. [33]

In Genesis 9:1 it says, "So God blessed Noah and his sons, and said to them: Be fruitful and multiply and fill the earth." God blessed Noah and his sons including Ham. To have cursed Ham, God would mean a violation of His covenant with Noah and Noah's sons (Gen. 9:1-17). God remains faithful to His covenant, even when we do not remain faithful (II Tim.. 2:13). Ham was not cursed, Ham was blessed (Gen. 9:1). Ham sinned by showing disrespect for his father, looking upon Noah's nakedness. God in his sovereignty cursed Canaan, not Ham, just as he punished Rehoboam instead of Solomon, out of respect for His covenant. Of Ham's four son's Canaan, the one who was cursed, no longer exist today as a nation!

We thank God that racist exegetes throughout history have distorted this text for their own selfish purposes. For therein, we can unravel the races of mankind in Scripture. They meant it for our evil but God meant it for our good. The curse of Ham theory did not curse us, but instead it gave us a compass through biblical trails to discover our presence in the Scripture. This compass leads us to the continent of Africa where we see Ham's sons creating great civilizations, before Europe was civilized. This compass leads us to Mesopotamia (Shinar-Babel) where we see the first world ruler and a mighty man who was a descendant of Ham-Nimrod. This compass leads us to the Nation of Israel being a mixed multitude (Ex. 12:38) having spent many years living in the land of Ham. This compass leads us all the way to the genealogy of Jesus Christ, where we find four Hamitic ladies in Jesus' family tree. We know the curse of Ham theory was meant for our evil, but God meant it for our good. Chuck Singleton was right,

The Word of God will straighten itself out even if it straightened around your neck.[34]

We do not believe that God would permit Jesus' return without revealing the truth about the races of mankind in history from a biblical perspective. All of these viewpoints, the scholarly opinions; the Tower of Babel theory; the devious, deceptive definitions; and the curse of Ham theory have been used to denigrate the identity and role of the Black man in Scripture. Now we want to move from defense to offense. Let us look at the other side of the argument.

NOTES
CHAPTER 5

1. "Ham," The International Standard Bible Encyclopedia, Wm. B. Eerdmans Publishing Co., Grand Rapids, MI, 1984, Vol. II, p. 1324.

2. William F. Albright, "The Old Testament World," in George Arthur Buttrick, ed., The Interpreter's Bible, Abingdon-Cokesbury Press, New York, 1952, p. 238.

3. "Ham," Pictorial Bible Dictionary, The Southwestern Company, Nashville, TN, 1975, p. 330.

4. Richard H. Popkin, "Hume's Racism," The Philosophical Forum, Vol. 9, Nos. 2-3, p. 213, quoted by Cornel West, Prophesy Deliverance!: An Afro-American Revolutionary Christianity, The Westminster Press, Philadelphia, 1982, p. 62 .

5. Arnold Toynbee, A Study of History, 1934, quoted by Indus Khamit Kush, What They Never Told You in History Class, Luxorr Publications, 1983, p. 2.

6. Winthrop Jordan, White Over Black: American Attitudes Toward the Negro, 1550-1812, W.W. Norton & Co., 1968, Pts. 1-3, esp. pp. 436-437, quoted by Cornel West, p. 62.

7. Popkin, p. 62.

8. C. L. Franklin, Give Me This Mountain: Life History and Selected Sermons, University of Illinois Press, Chicago, 1989, p. 187.

9. Frank M. Snowden, Jr., Before Color Prejudice: The Ancient View of Blacks, Harvard University Press, Cambridge, MA, 1983, p. 85.

10. Ibid., pp. 85-86.

11. Ibid., p. 87.

12. John Tierney, "The Search for Adam and Eve," Newsweek Magazine, January 11, 1988, pp. 46-52.

13. Rev. Robert E. Fowler reported this conversation in 1990 with a Southwestern Baptist Theological Seminary Professor.

14. Saint Augustine, The City of God, An Abridged Version from the Translation by Gerald G. Walsh, Demetrius B. Zema, Grace Monahan, and Daniel J. Honan, Image Books, Garden City, NY, 1958, p. 365.

15. Ibid., p. 271.

16. Ibid., p. 370.

17. Tierny, pp. 46-52.

18. "Caucasian," Webster's Students Dictionary, American Book Company, 1959, p. 130.

19. The New Lexicon Webster's Dictionary of the English Language, Lexicon Publications, Inc., New York, 1987, p. 156.

20. Ibid.

21. Ibid.

22. Ibid., p. 669.

23. Webster's Third New International Dictionary, G. & C. Merriam Company Publishers, Springfield, MA, 1971, p. 1024.

24. Ibid., p. 1210.

25. Ibid., p. 2065.

26. Funk & Wagnalls New Encyclopedia, Funk & Wagnalls Corp., New York, Vol. 12, p. 358.

27. "Caucasoid," Grolier Universal Encyclopedia, American Book-Stratford Press, Inc., New York, 1966, Vol. 2, p. 518.

28. Ibid.

29. Ed. by C.I. Scofield, The Scofield Reference Bible: The Holy Bible, Oxford University Press, New York, 1945, p. 16.

30. Smith's Bible Dictionary, Holman Bible Publishers, Nashville, 1991, rev. ed. compiled from Dr. William Smith's Dictionary of the Bible, p. 340.

31. Josephus: Complete Works, translated by William Whiston, Kregel Publications, Grand Rapids, MI, 1960, p. 31.

32. Arthur C. Custance, Noah's Three Sons: Human History in Three Dimensions, Vol. 1, The Doorway Papers, Zondervan Publishing House, Grand Rapids, MI, 1975, pp. 149-150.

33. Carlisle John Peterson, The Destiny of the Black Race, Lifeline Communications, Toronto, Canada, 1991, pp. 336-337.

34. Singleton, Sermon on Tape.

Chapter 6

BLACKS IN THE BIBLE: FACT OR FICTION

There are four basic arguments that we have chosen to present to document the plausibility of a pervasive and significant Black presence in Scripture. They are: (1) biblical and genetic insights; (2) linguistic, etymological, and genealogical evidence; (3) archaeological, anthropological and artistic clues; (4) scholarly and eyewitness testimonies. However, let us begin this section by defining what we mean by the term "Black".

As research is expanded on the subject of biblical and ancient ethnicity, we find more areas of agreement between Black and White scholars. Many White scholars admit that descendants of Japheth or Indo-Europeans played insignificant roles in the Old Testament. Some scholars will acknowledge, as Sayce does, that biblical characters were not "White" in the usual acceptance of the word. However, the significant disagreement between Black commentators and White commentators is in the coining of the races. As it relates to the biblical and ancient world, many Whites tend to adopt what we consider to be a devious or deceptive definition of Caucasians. This definition of "White" includes people who otherwise would be thought of as Blacks or people of color. As a matter of fact, White scholars have developed a definition for "White" or "Caucasian" that is broad enough for us to consider ourselves as "White." We have "dark brown" skin and "wooly hair", therefore we meet GROLIER'S encyclopedia's definition for "Caucasian". Yet, why are we not considered White? On a mug shot in America these people would be considered Black. However, in the biblical world they are somehow redefined as "Caucasians" or "Hamites". References are sometimes made of their fine "European features" - which means their complexion is not "jet black" and their features are not pronounced Negroid features.

Frank Snowden in his book BEFORE COLOR PREJUDICE commented:

Iconographical evidence has not been given enough weight in the assessment of the Black population. The tendency has been to give attention only to the so-called pure Negro and to ignore almost entirely blacks of less pronounced Negroid characteristics, with the result that the picture of Blacks in antiquity has been unrealistic and distorted as a study of the Black population in the United States or Brazil would be if restricted to a consideration of "pure Negroes".

Blacks in the Bible: Fact or Fiction 95

The works of artists that have come down to us are only a small fraction of what must have existed: all the more significant, then, are the large number and wide variety of Negroid types that have survived from every period of ancient art. If it is also kept in mind how often it is possible to relate the Blacks of ancient artists to specific facts or historical events, it is apparent that the value of iconography has been greatly underestimated. Though obviously much larger in Egypt than elsewhere, the Black population in other Mediterranean areas, especially in Northwest Africa and Italy, was probably also greater than traditional estimates. [1]

In modern history there is general agreement, at least in America, on the identification of a Black person. On the matter of ancient history there is no agreement on race identification. Therefore, the decision is often left to the personal bias of each writer or observer. It amazes us how many tend to see "European features" on people of color in the ancient world, but on people of color in America they see African features.

Our goal in dealing with this subject is to seek common-ground not battle-ground. Therefore, we are willing to refer to certain ancient biblical characters as "people of color" rather than "Blacks". We hope that White commentators are willing to make similar concessions. But as long as White commentators and the White media produce "Caucasian" Bible characters, we find it necessary to protest, for there were people of color included in the kaleidoscope of biblical characters and throughout the early church.

George Wells Parker, in his book THE CHILDREN OF THE SUN published in 1918, expressed the anger and frustration of Blacks who studied biblical and ancient ethnicity. They discovered that our history has been taken from us through devious and deceptive misapplication of "Caucasoid" or "Caucasian" classification.

> `What is history' once asked the great Napoleon, 'but a fiction agreed upon?' How truly has this agreement been kept by all American historians wherever the Black races have been concerned! With what pains have they undertaken to say certain people of antiquity were not Negroes and that Negroes appear upon the monuments of ancients as slaves only. ...what standing can such historians as Ridpath and Myers and others have with scholars when they classify the Ethiopians as a branch of the Caucasian race? Could the weeping Jeremiah but know that with a drop of ink an American has proven his logic faulty, he might then believe that a leopard can change its spots and those accustomed to do evil are capable of good. There is absolutely no grounds for such erroneous

statements in the light of modern science. They may call Herodotus the father of lies instead of the father of history; they may say that the author of Genesis had a weakness for genealogy and decided to settle the vexed questions of racial origins by writing faulty ancestral records; possible, too, that all other scribes and travelers suffered from diseases of mind and memory; but the tangible records in stone which these departed of earth's guests left behind them in token of their existence cannot be false. Whatever science has done or may do, one thing is certain: it has with indisputable evidence in stone and picture, established for all time that the African was the master and not the slave, the conqueror and not the conquered, the civilized and not the 'savage'. [2]

Black and White writers often reach different conclusions regarding biblical and ancient ethnicity. This is so, because they equate different definitions for the terms "Caucasian" and "Negro". Black American writers usually employ the bibliocentric (Genesis chapter ten) understanding of race. On the other hand, White writers employ the secret, inconsistent anthropological understanding of race, which in our opinion, is hypocritical and unbiblical. Their view somehow removes color as a determining factor in drawing racial conclusions. In America, color is the primary determining factor with regard to racial classification. As a matter of fact, any person with any traceable degree of Negro ancestry is classified as Black, although their skin color may be White. We are absolutely convinced that if European and Euro-American scholars apply the American understanding of race to the biblical world, we would be in complete agreement and harmony.

So, what is our definition for determining Blacks in the Bible? When discussing the issue of Blacks in the Bible, we must understand that the designation 'Black' is a term of accommodation. By accommodation, I mean that we are using twentieth-century terminology generated by a twentieth-century mind to discuss people who in some cases, lived more than two millennia ago. Thus, our distinctions are not necessarily their distinctions. Yet when we say "Black" in reference to those people of the past, we are on the one hand referring to physical traits African-Americans share with those people, namely skin color; on the other hand we are referring to the genetic lineage of African-Americans and its affinity with people of the ancient Near East and Egypt. ...descendants of African people do, beyond a doubt, have an ancestral linkage to certain critical personages in biblical history. [3]

Therefore, any dark complexioned person or nation in Scripture or ancient history, whose lineage can be traced to "Ham" or his descendants, will be defined as Black for the purposes of this work.

Biblical and Genetic Insights

The first argument that we will present in favor of a Black presence in Scripture is the biblical, genetic viewpoint. We will present evidence from Scripture and the laws of science (genetics) to explain the origin of all the races of mankind. Our focus will be on the origin of the Black, Negro, or African race.

Ken Ham, a Caucasian Australian and a creation research scientist, was the first man (besides Custance) that voiced a view of the origin of the races of mankind that was quite similar to what we have argued, although not identical. The following quote is taken directly from an official Radio Transcript with Ken Ham as the guest:

...Even the secular scientist today agrees that all people go back to one woman. ...They even call her Eve. They say African Eve, because they believe she evolved in Africa.

...Of course, a problem that some people then bring up is this: 'Well if we all came from Adam and Eve, how come there are different colored people in the world? Well, there aren't any different colored people; we're all the same color. If a black person was sitting beside me at the moment, that would be the same color as I am. They just have more of the color. It's a pigment called melanin in our skin. And Adam and Eve probably started with a fair bit of melanin--probably medium brown. The majority of the world's population today are medium brown, and some of their children could have been very dark--in fact, black through to light, in one generation. You know, some people get surprised at that but they shouldn't. For instance, I have at home in my desk a picture from a news paper which is headed 'Britain's Amazing Twins'--and one is white and the other is black, and they're twins. People wonder how that could be. Well, it just means one of them inherited genes with a little bit of melanin and the other one inherited genes with a lot of melanin, and there you have it. It's very easy to understand. And at the time of the Tower of Babel, in our history, when God gave different languages and people split up and went to different places on the earth's surface, then, of course, depending on which genes they took with them, would depend on which characteristics were dominant, and thus you get the various characteristics that are dominant features in the races we have in the world today, if you want to call them races, although races is not really a Biblical term. It's better to call them cultures or something like that. [4]

We do not teach, or necessarily believe, that Adam was Black. In our opinion, it is unfair to impose a twentieth century understanding of race on the first man who ever lived. However, we do believe Adam was a man of color having been formed from dirt on or near African soil (Genesis 2:7,13). Adam and Eve, we also believe, were genetically capable of producing the three basic races of mankind, solely apart from any climate or environment factors.

In a book that he co-authored called THE ANSWERS BOOK, Ken Ham provides genetic insights to explain the origin of the races of mankind.

> So you can see how it is easily possible, beginning with two middle-brown parents, to get not only all the colors, but also races with permanently different shades of coloring, ...we find that an entire range of color, from very white to very black, can result in only ONE GENERATION, beginning with this particular type of mid-brown parents. [5]

The key to understanding the biblical, genetic viewpoint is to understand the biblical records of man's origin and the races. It also calls for an understanding of the laws of genetics. Based on that fundamental understanding we can boldly say that Adam and Eve were medium brown in complexion, as Ken Ham also believes they were. We attribute their brown complexion to the soil from which they came, but Ken Ham attributes their complexion to a high level of melanin content. We all believe that Adam possessed the dominant genes and Eve possessed the recessive genes that rendered them capable of producing both dark and light-skinned children within one generation. According to Ken Ham, if the right combination of genes is held by both parents, then two dark people, or a dark and a light person can produce a variety of colors. Ken Ham wrote:

> It has long been known that if people of mulatto descent marry, their offspring may be virtually any color, ranging from very black to very white. [6]

We encourage the reading and study of Ken Ham's book, THE ANSWERS BOOK, and his official radio interview transcript, "SCIENCE, SCRIPTURE AND SALVATION." He supports the genetic theory to prove the various colors of mankind in opposition to the climatic or environmental theories. And regarding the Tower of Babel theory, Ken Ham believes it played a significant role in racial segregation. Thus, racial segregation caused more pronounced features of one group as opposed to a group with mixed genes. Color variation existed in just one generation after Adam as is evident by Ham's color. Mid-brown or mulattoes were the dominant color before the Tower of Babel and the flood, with the very dark and the very light skinned persons in existence. According to Ken Ham, the post flood and pre-Babel population groups were similar with regard to skin color. [7]

> After the flood, for the few centuries until Babel, there was only one language and one culture group. Thus there were no barriers to marriage within this group. This would tend to keep the skin color of the population away from the extremes. Very dark and very light skin would appear, of course, but people tending in either direction would be free to marry someone less dark or less light than themselves, ensuring that the average color would roughly stay the same. The same would be true of other characteristics, not just skin color. Under these sorts of circumstances, distinct racial lines will never emerge. This is true for animals as well as human populations, as every biologist knows. To obtain such separate lines, you would need to break a large breeding group into smaller groups and keep them separate, that is, not interbreeding any more. [8]

Again, if Ken Ham is correct, the Pre-Flood and Pre-Babel biblical world was made up of primarily people of medium brown complexion, with the very light and very dark also present. This was probably the only period in history when race prejudice truly did not exist from any angle. Although we believe that variety of colors in the races of mankind which exist today, existed before the flood, the pre-flood inhabitants saw themselves as--one race--the human family.

The noted White Bible commentator, Finnis Dake wrote of Noah's race:

> All colors and types of men came into existence after the flood. All men were White up to this point, for there was only one family line-- that of Noah who was White and in the line of Christ. [9]

But there are other claims regarding the color of Noah and his fellow inhabitants. Ken Ham wrote a refreshing argument:

> Noah and his family were probably mid-brown, with genes for both dark and light skin, because a medium skin color (dark enough to protect against skin cancer, yet light enough to allow vitamin D production) would be the most suitable in the world before the

Flood. (It is likely that there were then no harsh extremes of climate). As all the factors for skin color were present in Adam and Eve, they would most likely have been mid-brown as well. [10]

We also believe that the factors of skin color originated with Adam, though, we do not believe Adam was Black. For instance, Adam could have been a man of color similar to the late Andwar Sadat of Egypt. We recognize a parallel between the location of the Garden of Eden, near Ethiopia (Genesis 2:13), and that Ethiopians consider themselves the first people on the face of the earth. Diodorus of Sicily wrote,

> The Ethiopians call themselves the first of all men and cite proofs they consider evident. It is generally agreed that, born in a country and not having come from elsewhere, they must be judged indigenous. It is likely that located directly under the course of the sun, they sprang from the earth before other men. For if the heat of the sun, combining with the humidity of the soil, produces life, those sites nearest the Equator must have produced living beings earlier than others... [11]

Even if Adam was formed from African soil, specifically Ethiopian soil, that still may not be the reason to classify him as Black. Dr. W.E.B. Dubois in his book entitled THE NEGRO, makes the following comment regarding the complexion of primitive Africans:

> The primitive African was not an extreme type. One may judge from modern pygmy and Bushmen that his color was reddish or yellow, and his skull was sometimes round like the Mongolian." [12]

The main points are: Adam was made from the soil. He was probably formed on African soil. His complexion was dark to medium-brown. It would be unfair to classify him racially, though he may possibly have been Semitic; because his chronological record places him in the family of Noah and Shem (Luke 3:36-38).

Let us return to the complexion of Noah and his sons. We believe that Noah and his wife were brown-skinned people as Ken Ham stated. We also believe very light people (as Europeans), and very dark people (as Africans), existed during the pre-flood and post-flood days. Why? Because Adam and Eve were genetically capable of producing sundry colors along with their descendants, so inevitably, it did happen.

On June 17, 1993, on Channel 27 in Dallas, Texas, the Sally Jesse Raphael Show featured three Black women. Although one of the women was intensely dark in complexion, all three women bore children who appeared White. It was very remarkable, so much so, that the women had to convince people that the children were their biological offsprings. In Ken Ham's, THE ANSWERS BOOK, he reproduced a picture appearing in an Australian newspaper that featured a Nigerian woman married to a British man. [13] The Nigerian woman had typical African features--the British man had typical European features. This couple produced twins. One child emerged with typical Nigerian features; while the other emerged with typical European features. The caption beneath the pictures reads:

Meet Britain's most amazing twins--in black and white. Thomas is black and Wesley is white. [14]

Ken Ham commented: "A fascinating mix of genes. Mandy and Tom Charnock gave birth to twins--one white, one black."[15] Although it is not a very common occurrence in our day and time, it is not without credence that an inter-racial couple can produce children with features reflecting either parent. Hence, it was quite possible during the days of Noah.

Noah named his sons Ham, Shem and Japheth. According to the INTERNATIONAL STANDARD BIBLE ENCYCLOPEDIA, 1956 edition, in its discussion of "Ham" we learn the following about the names of Noah's sons:

As Shem means "dusky," or the like, and Japheth "fair," it has been supposed that Ham meant, as is not improbable, "black." This is supported by evidence of [Hebrew] and [Arabian], in which the word "haman" means "to be hot" and "to be black," the latter signification being derived from the former. [16]

One might say Noah nicknamed his sons, "Shem" - dusky, "Japheth" - fair, and "Ham"- black. Based on observation or Divine revelation, Noah saw the complexion of his sons and their descendants and thus named them to suit.

Noah's descendants correspond with certain racial groupings which correspond directly with the modern day understanding of race. The Pictorial Bible Dictionary states:

...archaeology have found Hamitic artifacts under Semitic ruins of Assyrian cities. Shem, Ham, and Japheth probably differed only as brothers do, but their descendants are quite distinct. [17]

Was Noah's sons born with color distinctions, or did color distinctions evolve later in their descendants? One cannot speak dogmatically on this question unless an eyewitness; but we certainly believe Noah visually or prophetically saw these color distinctions in his sons. It is scientifically or genetically possible for Noah and his wife to have produced sons with three distinct complexions. According to Burnett Hanson, M.D., it is possible for a man to father three children with three different complexions--one "black or dark," another "dusky" or olive-colored," and the third "bright or fair"--by the same woman. Dr. Hanson further adds, "In order for this to take place, either the man or the wife has to be dark complexioned or both of them could have been dark. Dark-skinned people can and often do produce fair offsprings. However, it is genetically impossible for fair people to produce dark-skinned children." Dr. Hanson concluded that in order for Noah to have fathered three sons by the same woman, with all three sons having distinct complexions ranging from dark to bright, Noah or his wife had to be black or dark-skinned. [18]

Dr. Hanson's analysis is correlative to Ken Ham's analysis:

> We know that skin color is governed by at least two (possibly more) sets of genes. Let's call them A and B, with the correspondingly more silent genes a and b...Let's look at what combination would result in a mulatto (the offspring of an AA BB and aa bb). Surprisingly, we find that an entire range of color, from very white to very black, can result in only ONE GENERATION, beginning with this particular type of mid-brown parents. [19]

Based on the above analysis, it is quite easy for us to believe that Noah's sons reflected the complexions that their names indicate. Unquestionably, their descendants did. It could very well be that after the Tower of Babel the descendants of each of Noah's sons segregated unto themselves. Due to a diminished pool of gene mixing and the effects of the environment, existing physical features became more pronounced. We are fully persuaded that when the descendants of Noah gathered at Babel, racial distinctions were already clearly in place.

In reference to the climatic, environmental view, it would take two to three thousand years for the sun to change a race of people to Black or the cold weather to turn a race to White. But genetically it could take only one generation. "Whose report is more believable?" The Tower of Babel theorist, or the inerrant Word of God Who said, "God hath taken one blood and made all nations of men" (Acts 17:26 KJV).

The biblical genetic viewpoint underscores our belief that Ham inherited his darkness the same way all children derive their color from their parents. And Ham's parents inherited their complexions from Adam and Eve, from whom all people on the face of the earth received their color. "Red and yellow, black and white, we're all precious in God's sight."

Adam and Eve were capable of producing the various complexions found on the face of the earth without any help from the sun. Why is it that fundamentalist Christians would rather believe the Tower of Babel or Environment Theory, rather than the biblical and genetic truth regarding the origin of the races of mankind? The Tower of Babel theory is not taught in Scripture. The biblical and Genetic truth is taught in Scripture and is affirmed as a plausible viewpoint based on the laws of science (genetics). The latter is a more simple and reasonable explanation than the Tower of Babel theory and is inclusive of all mankind in biblical history. The Tower of Babel Theory endows only Whites a pre-Babel biblical heritage.

In 1879, a Black physician named Martin R. Delany, of Charleston, South Carolina, published a book entitled THE ORIGIN OF RACES AND COLOR. Delany's argument and conclusions provide an explanation for the various races of mankind, primarily based on genetics. His viewpoint is quite similar to Ken Ham's, although not identical. Delany's writings can be described as strongly Bibliocentric and Afrocentric. Because Delany's book is not easily accessible, we want to give ample testimony to his arguments and interact with them along the way. In the book's Preface Delany wrote,

> ...the two extremes of color, from the most negative white--'including every possible variety of tint'--up to the blackest are all produced by the same material and essential properties of color. [20]

In chapter one of his book, Delany stated his belief that the Bible is an authoritative source. He also stated his rejection of the "Development theory" [meaning The Tower of Babel and the Environment theory] and the "Three creations theory" [which was apparently popular in Delany's day]. He wrote:

> ...accepting the Mosaic or Bible Record, as our basis, without an allusion to the Development theory.

> The theory of Champollion, Nott, Gliddon, and others of the Three Creations of man; one Black, the second yellow, and the last White, we discard, and shall not combat as theory.... We have named these Three Races, in the order which they are said to have been created, the Black being first, consequently the oldest of the human family. [21]

We find it noteworthy that the French Champollion brothers, Jean the Egyptologist (1790-1832), and Jacques Champollion, the philologist (1778-1867), both believed, according to Delany, that the Black man was created first. Champollion's belief coincides with H.G.Wells who stated, "Possibly the more ancient races of men were all dusky or Black and fairness is new." [22] Even A.H. Sayce, the Oxford philologist and ethnologist, wrote: "It is probable that dark skin was characteristic of primitive man." [23]

Delany's belief in the reliability of Scripture is constant. He affirmed:

> In treating on the Unity of Races as descended from one parentage, we shall make no apology for a liberal use of Creation as learned from the Bible. In this, we find abundant proof to sustain the position in favor of the Unity of the Human Race. [Bear in mind, Delany was a medical doctor, a dedicated Christian, and a serious student of the Bible when he addressed these issues. His perspectives were unique, particularly, at the time he wrote them.][24]

In chapters two and three, Delany presented his rationale for the various complexions of mankind. He apportioned all complexions to Adam, and not to the sun.

> Man, according to Biblical history, commenced his existence in the Creation of Adam. [25]

> There is no doubt that, until the entry into the Ark of the Family of Noah, the people were all of the "One Race" and Complexion; which leads us to further inquiry, What was that complexion?

> It is, we believe, generally admitted among linguists, that the Hebrew word Adam (ahdam) signifies red-dark red as some scholars have it. And it is, we believe, a well settled admission that the name of the Original Man, was taken from his complexion. [26]

Delany believed that Adam's complexion was the color of clay or yellowish, similar to pure-blooded "North American Indians." He further believed that all the people from Adam to Noah, including Noah's wife and his son's wives, were all the same color. However, he believed Noah's sons had different colors and their descendants gathered at the Tower of Babel. Delany wrote:

> There is to us another fact of as little doubt: that is, that these sons of Noah all differed in complexion...their dependents in and about the city and around about the Tower also differed as did the three sons in complexion.... That Shem was of the same complexion of Noah his father, and another - the Adamic complexion - there is no doubt in our mind. And that Ham the second son was swarthy in

complexion, we have as little doubt. Indeed, we believe that it is generally conceded by scholars, though disputed by some, that the word Ham means 'dark,' 'swarthy,' 'sable.' And it has always been conceded, and never as we know seriously disputed that Japheth was White. [27]

How did the various colors originate? First, Delany argued that in the animal kingdom and vegetable reproduction (including botany) it is not uncommon for one source to produce a variety, or at least a variable color. Secondly, he argued that all people regardless of their complexions have varying degrees of rouge [a coloring matter-the essential properties which give redness to rose according to Delany] in their bodies. Delany stated that:

> Thus the color of the blackest African is produced by identically the same essential coloring matter that gives the 'rosy cheeks and ruby lips,' to the fairest and most delicately beautiful white lady. [28]

Delany probably drew the following illustration from his medical laboratory.

> For illustration, to prove that concentrated rouge or concrete redness is black, take blood caught in a vessel, let it cool and dry up by evaporation of the liquid part; when condensed in a solid mass, it becomes perfectly black, more so than the blackest human being ever seen. [29]

So, How did Noah's three sons get there three colors? Delany explains it thusly:

> Here we see that the first son of Noah, Shem, was born with a high degree of a certain complexion or color; the second son, Ham, with a higher degree, or intensity of the same color, making a different complexion; and the third son, Japheth, with the least of the same color, which gives an entirely different complexion to either. These three brothers were all same color - rouge -which being possessed in different degrees simply, gave them different complexions.

> Was there any miracle in this; any departure from the regular order of the laws of nature, necessary to the production of these three sons of a different complexion by the same mother and father of one complexion? Certainly not; as it is common to see parents of one complexion, and hair and eyes of one color, produce children with hair and eyes of various colors. Then the same laws in physiology,

which produced the former of these variations, also produced the other; but for His all - wise purposes - doubtless the production of fixed races of man - the effect was placed upon the skin instead of the eyes and hair. [30]

Ken Ham and Martin Delany, were both conservative, evangelical, scholarly Christians. They wrote in separate centuries; one White and the other Black. They both provided for the body of Christ, biblical and scientifically plausible explanations for the various colors of the races of mankind—without denigrating either race.

Arthur Custance, the evangelical Canadian scholar, also believed that Ham was a man of dark color. In his book, NOAH'S THREE SON'S, published by Zondervan Press, Custance claimed:

> Without becoming involved in the technicalities of genetics it is possible that Ham may himself have been a mulatto. In fact, his name means "dark" and perhaps refers to the color of his skin. This condition may have been derived, through his mother, Noah's wife, and if we suppose that Ham had himself married a mulatto woman, it is possible to account for the preservation of the Negroid stock over the disaster of the flood. [31]

Custance's reference to the "technicalities of genetics" suggest that he believed it was possible to explain Ham's darkness based on genetic factors as opposed to environmental or climatic factors.

The biblical, genetic viewpoint, summarized, is that through the loins and genes of Adam, and particularly through the sons of Noah, the three basic races of mankind emerged, prior to the Tower of Babel. These races segregated themselves after the Tower of Babel and became identified as "the sons of Ham," "the sons of Shem" and "the sons of Japheth." Each group inherited certain physical features from the progenitor of their respective tribe. From Ham came the dark races, from Shem came the non-Hamitic dusky and olive races and from Japheth came the fairest people.

Herein lies the basis for the Black, White, and Semitic presence in Scripture.

If Black and White Christian leaders would examine this subject objectively, we believe that we could debunk the Tower of Babel and the Environment theory in one generation. The end result would be, the truth, broadcasted to the people of color to eliminate the implied teaching that Blacks came into existence coincidentally. We would also debunk the myth that Whites have ruled this world since its inception. The Black presence in Scripture is in part based on the biblical, genetic viewpoint.

Linguistic, Etymological and Genealogical Evidence

The presence of Blacks in the Bible can also be documented through Etymological and Genealogical Evidence. Etymology is simply the study of words; their origin, meaning, and derivations. With regard to color designation, names are actually used to refer to the actual skin tone of dark people. Let us begin by studying the word "Ham" through the eyes of capable scholars.

THE INTERNATIONAL STANDARD BIBLE ENCYCLOPE-DIA stated the following definition of "Ham":

> The name given, in Psalms 105: 23,27; 106:22(cf 78:51), to Egypt as a descendant of Ham, son of Noah. ...it has been supposed that Ham meant, as is not improbable, "black." This is supported by evidence of Heb[rew] and Arab[ic], in which the word "haman" means "to be hot" and "to be black," the later signification being derived from the former. [32]

FAUSSET'S BIBLE DICTIONARY published by Zondervan Press gave this definition for Ham:

> Ham = hot. 1. The Egyptian Kem (Egypt peculiarly the land of Ham, Psalm 1xxviii.51, ev.23), "black"; the sunburnt and those who[sic] soil is black, as Ethiopia means. ...The first steps in the arts and sciences seemingly are due to the Hamites. The earliest empires were theirs, their power of organization being great... [33]

The entry for "Egypt", Fausset's made the following relative comments to our subject matter:

> Egypt. The genealogies in Gen.X. concern races, not mere descent of persons....The hieroglyphic name for Egypt is Kem, "black," alluding to its black soil, combining also the idea of heat, 'the hot dark country'. The cognate Arabic word means 'black mud.' Ham is perhaps the same name, prophetically descriptive of 'the land of Ham' (Psalm cv.23,27). ...Origin - The Egyptians were of Nigritian origin. [34]

There are many who reject the claim that Ham means "black" in Hebrew. According to ISBE Shem means "dusky," and Japheth means "fair". But for one reason or another, some scholars argue against the meaning of "Ham" to mean "black" in Hebrew, and they may be right.

Now, some argue against a etymological relationship between the Hebrew "Ham" and the Egyptian "Kem." The late, great African scholar C.A. Diop, who earned his Master of Arts and his doctorate from the University of Paris, bridged the gap between the scholars. Nobody disputes that the Egyptian name Kem, or KMT, means "black" or "swarthy"; but there is a question whether Ham in Hebrew means "black." Diop wrote:

> Whence came this name Ham (Cham, Kam)? Where could Moses have found it? Right in Egypt where Moses was born, grew up, and lived until Exodus. In fact, we know that the Egyptians called their country Kemit, which means "black" in their language. The interpretation according to which Kemit designates the black soil of Egypt, rather than the black man and, by extension, the black race of the country of Blacks, stems from the gratuitous distortion by minds aware of what an exact interpretation of this word would imply. Hence, it is natural to find Kam in Hebrew, meaning heat, black, burned. [35]

Moses, the author of Genesis, Hebrew or Semitic by race, was trained in all the learning of the Egyptians (Acts 7:22). He was indeed raised in Pharaoh's house and spoke Pharaoh's language (Egyptian). Now, since Moses viewed the Hebrew "Ham" and the Egyptian "Kem" as synonyms, then there should be no disagreement between the meaning of the words today. Furthermore, if the etymology of "Japheth" and "Shem" were used by Noah and Moses to denote color, would it not be reasonable to conclude that when they used the name "Ham" it denoted a color designation.

Additionally, how do we know the language of Noah? Languages, as we know them, did not come into existence until after the Tower of Babel. The pre-Babel language is a matter of much debate. So who can say with certainty that the word "Ham" did not mean "black" in the language of Noah when he named his sons?

If civilization originated in Africa (as some writers claim) it is not unreasonable to assume that languages began in Africa. It is interesting that certain African tribes up to this day trace their roots back to a man named "Ham." According to Custance, the Yoruba tribe traces their roots to Nimrod, Ham's descendant.

Noah was a part of the pre flood civilization which began near Ethiopia. The noted linguist, Joseph Greenberg stated, "the long dead mother tongue of all these languages [Semitic, Hebrew, Arabic, Phoenician, Aramaic, Amharic, Hamitic, Egyptian, Cushitic, Chadic and Hausa] would have originated in the highlands of Ethiopia. [36] What this means, in effect, is that the Semitic languages are branches of an original northeast African parent, of which Egyptian and Cushitic are stems. Cornell Professor, Martin Bernal, in his book, BLACK ATHENA: THE AFROASIATIC ROOTS OF CLASSICAL CIVILIZATION, Volume I, asserted the origin of languages that is parallel to Greenberg's assertion:

> It is generally agreed that the Greek language was formed during the 17th and 16th centuries B.C. Its Indo-European structure and basic lexicon are combined with a non-Indo-European vocabulary of sophistication. I am convinced that much of the latter can be plausibly derived from Egyptian and West Semitic. This would fit very well with a long period of domination by Egypto-Semitic conquerors. [37]

The point is Noah probably spoke in "the long dead mother tongue of all these languages" according to Greenberg's reference. Who among us can tell us that Ham did not mean "black" in the "long dead mother tongue that Noah spoke?" The "long dead mother tongue" of Ethiopia, somehow became a part of all the existing languages which Greenberg referenced and the roots of which Bernal traced to the Indo-European languages into Egypt. Furthermore, even if Noah spoke a Semitic or Hebrew language (which is highly unlikely since the Hamitic language preceded the Semitic languages); it is well known that there is a strong relationship between Semitic and Hamitic, Egyptian, Cushitic, and Ethiopian Chadic languages. A NEW STANDARD BIBLE DICTIONARY in a section called "Ethnography and Ethnology" reported on the linguistic and social relationship between Hamites and Semites:

> The Hamites and Semites have very strongly marked characteristics - linguistic and social, if not physical - which justify grouping them in this manner. Both Hamitic and Semitic languages have consonant roots - former predominately bi-lateral and quadri-lateral, the later tri-lateral - and certain peculiar laryngeal and velar sounds; and show indubitable agreement in inflection, if not in vocabulary. Many obscure phenomena in Semitic languages, such as the odd uses of the feminine, the reversal of gender with certain numerals, and the so called broken plurals, are easily explained from Hamitic. [38]

For those who claim that one cannot draw inferences regarding the color of Ham based on the etymology of his name, we strongly disagree. For those who claim that Ham does not mean "black" we argue that it is impossible to know what Noah and Moses had in mind. Noah may have spoken the name "Ham", in the "long dead mother tongue" of Ethiopia. So, we have to argue and reason from the languages we do know. And here is what we do know regarding the ethnicity and etymology of Ham.

■ It was genetically possible for Ham to have been born dark or Black.

■ We know his brothers bore names which reflected color designations. So there is no reason why Ham's name should not also reflect a color designation.

■ Moses spoke the Hebrew and Egyptian languages and he was very familiar with the Egyptian word Kem meaning black. It is therefore possible that when Moses recorded Ham's name in the book of Genesis, he was simply using the Hebrew equivalent of Kem. And if he was using the Hebrew equivalent, it was then Moses who first taught racial grouping in Scripture.

■ Perhaps if it were not so easy to trace and identify racial groups in chapter ten of Genesis, we may be inclined to agree with those who say that it was not Moses' intent to classify race. But the mere fact that archaeology and ancient testimonies confirm that each person listed as a son of Ham was Black or dark, certainly suggests that their father (Ham) had to be Black or dark. For those who credit Japheth as the father of the Europeans; or Caucasians and Shem as the father of the Semitic people (Jews and Arabs); why are the Africans and people of color denied the privilege of claiming Ham as their progenitor?

■ When Josephus referred to, "The children of Ham", what did he have in mind? Certainly, when he discussed the Table of Nations in the tenth chapter of Genesis, neither Josephus or Moses saw it necessary to qualify that the sons of Japheth, Shem, and Ham were physically different in color.[39] That was a given for these must have been distinguishing factors between their descendants. And the names of their progenitors indicated that the distinctions were in their complexions. Race inter-relations was commonplace between the Hamites and Semites. Consequently, they were oftentimes physically, linguistically, and socially indistinguishable (Acts 21:38).

Dr. Charles Finch of Atlanta possesses a trustworthy scholarship, and for us, he confirms and settles the question of whether Ham means "Black." In his endnotes, Finch cites E.A.W. Budge's AN EGYPTIAN HIEROGLYPHIC DICTIONARY as his source. Finch wrote,

Our name "Ham" comes from the Hebrew word 'cham' which in turn is derived from the Egyptian word KAM, meaning 'black.'[40]

We could allege many other scholars who agree that Ham means "dark" or "Black"; but the point has been sufficiently stated.

Not only can we trace that Ham was Black through the meaning of his name but we can also trace the Black presence in Scripture through the biblical names of Cush, Kedar, Niger, and Phut. All the descendants listed in Genesis 10:6-20, in the family of Ham would be considered Black. Through inter-marriages, some of those groups have lost their distinct Hamitic features. Nevertheless, the Black presence in Scripture can be traced through the man and his name--"Ham".

When the matter of Blacks in the Bible was taught to a certain Black congregation, one lady described the Black race as a "bunch of hams." That was a comical way of putting it, but we believe that dark-skinned people throughout the world are descendants of Ham - thus, making us "all a bunch of Hams."

Archaeological, Anthropological and Artistic Clues

Archaeological, anthropological and artistic studies of the biblical and ancient world, reveal a significant Black presence in Scripture. The following references authenticate the Black presence in Scripture through an overwhelming number of artifacts and anthropological conclusions.

A. Raymond Woolsey, a White author, in his book, MEN AND WOMEN OF COLOR IN THE BIBLE, reported on iconographical documentation that at least three of Ham's descendants (Gen. 10:6) were dark-skinned people:

> In a wall painting from an Egyptian tomb dating from the four-teenth century B.C., some ancient artist depicted several races of people, all lined up. There are the Cushites, black-skinned; then the 'Asiatics' or Canaanites, pictured as dark brown; and the Egyptian themselves, a reddish brown. [41]

B. Earnest C. Sargent III, in his book MAJESTIC HONOR, has recorded information about the complexions of Ham's four sons as reflected on the "tomb of Sefi, c. 1300 B.C." Sargent wrote:

> The Egyptians are depicted as a brown skinned people. The Canaanites are pictured as tan or yellow in color. The Libyans appear almost white in color, while the Cushites are depicted as jet black (VIEWS OF THE BIBLICAL WORLD, p. 38, 39). [42]

C. In commenting on the color variations within the Hamitic family, Arthur C. Custance in his book, NOAH'S THREE SONS, confirmed:

There are other native African tribes which trace themselves back traditionally to Ham. The Yoruba who are black skinned, for example, claim to be descendants of Nimrod, whereas the Libyans, who are 'white skinned' [Berbers], are usually traced back to Lehabim, a son of Mizraim, and the Egyptians were direct descendants of Mizraim. It is therefore possible that all of Africa, despite the different shades of colors of its native populations, was initially settled by various members of this one Hamitic family. [43]

The Berbers seem to be an indigenous light-skinned people, although, certainly not as light as Europeans who lived in North Africa (Libya) from the beginning of time.

D. Alexander Hislop, a European antiquarian, in his book THE TWO BABYLONS affirmed that Nimrod (Gen. 10:8-12), a descendant of Ham, was worshipped as a god in Assyria, Egypt, and Greece. Nimrod was depicted in ancient and classical art as a Negro. Hislop reported:

Thus from Assyria, Egypt, and Greece we have cumulative and overwhelming evidence, all conspiring to demonstrate that the child worshipped in the arms of the goddess-mother in all these countries is the very character of Ninus or Nin, 'The Son,' was Nimrod, the son of Cush....

The amazing extent of the worship of this man indicates something very extraordinary in his character; and there is ample reason to believe, that in his own day he was an object of high popularity....

Now Nimrod, as the son of Cush, was Black, in other words was a Negro."

Semiramis gained glory from her dead and deified husband [Nimrod]; and in course of time both of them, under the names of Rhea and Nin, or 'Goddess-Mother and Son,' were worshipped with an enthusiasm that was incredible, and their images were set up and adored. Wherever the Negro aspect of Nimrod was found an obstacle to his worship, this was very easily obviated. According to the Chaldean doctrine of the transmigration of the souls, all that was needful was just to teach that Ninus [Nimrod] had reappeared in the person of a posthumous son, of a fair complexion, supernaturally borne by his widowed wife after the father had gone to glory. [44]

Hislop further added concerning the Caucasian's worship of a Negro:

It is wonderful to find in what widely severed countries, and amongst what millions of the human race at this day, who never saw a Negro, a negro god is worshipped. [45]

The major point is that Nimrod was viewed as a Negro by the classical world, and was depicted as such in ancient art, according to Hislop. Yet, the majority of White scholars in our day and time deny that Ham and his descendants, including Nimrod, were Black or Negroid. We find this baffling and unsettling in light of a preponderance of evidence that contradicts the modern widespread opinion by White scholars, which maintains the Hamites were not Black.

E. The great Black historian, W.E.B. Dubois, who earned his Ph.D. in history from Harvard University, revealed these anthropological and archaeological insights in his book called, THE NEGRO:

...it is certainly proved to-day beyond doubt that the so called Hamites of Africa, the brown and black curly and frizzly-haired inhabitants of North and East Africa, are not 'White men' if we draw the line between White and Black in any logical way.

Ancient statues of Indian divinities show the Negro type with a black face and close-curled hair, and early Babylonian culture was Negroid. In Arabia the Negroes may have been divided, and one stream perhaps wandered into Europe by way of Syria. Traces of these Negroes are manifest not only in skeletons, but in the brunette type of all South Europe. The other branch proceeded to Egypt and tropical Africa. ...most ancient skulls of Algeria are Negroid. ...Egyptian monuments show distinctly Negro and mulatto faces. ...The great Sphinx at Gizeh, so familiar to all the world, the Sphinxes of Tanis, the statue from the Fayum, ...all represent black, full blooded Negroes...described by Petrie as 'having high cheek bones, flat cheeks, both in one plane, a massive nose, firm projecting lips, and thick hair, with an austere, and almost savage expression of power. ...Black priests appear in Crete three thousand years before Christ [Most scholars equate Crete with the biblical Caphtorim (Gen. 10:14); thus, placing the original inhabitants of Crete in the family of Ham].[46]

F. Margaret Oliphant, in her book THE ATLAS OF THE ANCIENT WORLD captured in illustration, two ancient relics seldom associated with Negroes in biblical lands.

(1) Pyramids in Egypt are well known but pyramids in what is called "black Africa" are not well known. In her book, Oliphant featured a Nubian pyramid at Meroe, "smaller at the base and taller in proportion than Egyptian ones.[47] She stated, "The Nubians are dark skinned."

(2) Oliphant pictured an eighth century B.C. ivory artifact, where a Nubian is attacked by a lioness in the Assyrian city (still in existence today named Nimrod. The caption stated:

> A Nubian is attacked by a lioness in this gilded Phoenician ivory, which was used as an inlay in furniture. The ivory was one of a pair found in the Assyrian city of Nimrud [Nimrod]. It dates from the eighth century B.C. when quantities of Phoenician and Syrian ivories were plundered by Assyrians.[48]

We appreciate the acknowledgement of Oliphant that the man on the artifact was a Nubian. However, since Hamites were natives of Asshur [Assyria] according to Genesis 10:11, it is also possible that the man on the artifact could have been Assyrian or Phoenician. Both were in the family of Ham. THE PICTORIAL BIBLE DICTIONARY stated, "archaeologist have found Hamitic artifacts under semitic ruins of Assyrian cities."[49] Could the "Nubian" be one of the "Hamitic artifacts" which proves that Assyria was occupied by Hamites before the Semites took over?

Thus far, the ichnographical evidence is sufficiently convincing that Ham was Black. However, let us return briefly to the etymological conclusions that will lead us to anthropological conclusions.

The Oxford philologist, A.H. Sayce, disagrees with the notion of drawing racial inferences from the etymology of Noah's sons. He considers such attempts to be a "very doubtful value," but he does not refute the accuracy of the name translations of Noah's sons. That is "Japheth" meaning "White", and "Shem" meaning "olive-colored." Sayce affirmed the translation of Noah's son--Cham "to be hot" but he believed that the latter translation in no way indicated that "Cham" or "Ham" meant "black", directly or indirectly. In his book RACES OF THE OLD TES-TAMENT Sayce writes,

> Attempts have been made to explain the names of the three sons of Noah as referring to the color of the skin. Japheth has been com-pared with the Assyrian ippatu 'white,'Shem with the Assyrian samu 'olive colored,' while in Ham etymologist have seen the Hebrew Kham 'to be hot.' But all such attempts are of very doubtful value. It is, for instance, a long stride from the meaning of 'heat' to that of 'blackness'--a meaning of 'heat' to that of 'blackness'--a meaning,

indeed, which the Hebrew word never bears. Moreover, 'the sons of Ham' were none of them black-skinned, with the possible exception of a part of the population of Cush. Prof. Virchow has shown that the Egyptian, like the Canaanite, belongs to the white race, his red skin being merely the result of sunburn. [50]

Sayce's in his book also stated that all the biblical races were White. Therefore, it would be impossible for Sayce to conclude that the etymology of Noah's sons names were indicative of the dominant complexions of their descendants. [51] There is enough evidence adduced inadvertently in Sayce's book, to disprove his view that the etymology of the names of Noah's sons were not intended to denote the racial compositions of their descendants. To support his analysis, Sayce claimed that none of the sons of Ham were "black-skinned." Nothing could be farther from the truth. The Hamites were the darkest of Noah's sons, and this is reflected on Egyptian monuments. The Hebrew word for "black" to denote a color or race distinction is "Cush." Nobody debates the fact that Cush means "black' in Hebrew. How could Moses have used the Hebrew name, "Cush," to denote "Ham's" color, if Ham's first born son was also named "Cush" (Gen. 10:6)? This would have been very confusing. There was not another word Moses could have used other than the word Noah used; and the word that appeared to be synonymous with the Egyptian word "Kem" or "Kmt" meaning "black".

Cornell professor, Martin Bernal, rendered the following interpretation and insight regarding "KMT" and the color of black in Egypt. He wrote:

...black was also the national color of Egypt. Kmt (the black land) meant 'Egypt' and Kmt with the determinative for 'people' meant Egyptians." [The people and the land of Egypt were referred to by the Egyptians as "Kmt" meaning black, which was a reference to their dominant complexions (particularly at the dawn of post flood civilization) and their land.] [52]

Ham was named by Noah. Moses derived the name "Kem", or "Kmt", from Egypt and also "Ham" from the oral tradition of the Hebrews. The Egyptians got the name "Ham" or "Kem" from Ham. Furthermore, the Bible refers to Egypt as "the land of Ham" (Psalms 105:23).

In comparison, when reading Sayce's analysis of the etymology of Noah's sons, quoted above, it amazes us as to the length some writers will go to remove Blacks from the Bible. Since Sayce and others denied that Ham meant Black and the Hamites were Black, this is probably why W.E.B. Dubois rejected this term. The retired African-American Stanford

University Professor, St. Clair Drake, shares Dubois' frustration with the term "Hamite." Drake wrote:

> It is a matter of taxonomical irony that, by the time Dubois wrote THE NEGRO, anthropologist had taken a word that was used during the period of slavery to mean, 'an inferior breed of humanity descended from Ham, that is, a Negro,' and transformed it to mean 'a light-skinned African with Caucasian features, definitely superior to darker Africans, especially Negroid ones." Dubois assailed the use of the term 'Hamite,' under cover of which millions of Negroids have been characteristically transferred to the 'white'race by some eager scientist.' [53]

Drake then identified two anthropological questions that we also challenge theological academia to answer:

> Black Americans with an interest in this issue asked two perfectly logical questions that drew evasive answers from physical anthropologist, wrapped up in technical jargon: 'Why are people who look like us called 'white' or 'Hamite' if they live in Egypt but 'Negroes' if they live in this country?' and 'Why, if someone of that type turns up among the Egyptian pharaohs is he classified 'white,' but if he lived in Mississippi he'd be put in the back of the bus?' Dubois and other vindicationists were led to adopt a simple basic strategy. They called for consistency in the use of the term 'Negro.' They pointed out that failure to do so automatically removed virtually all of Egypt's achievements from the realm of the Black World. [54] [And might we add, failure to do so removes Blacks from the biblical world]

G. In response to Sayce's belief that the biblical world was made up of Whites only, we want to apprehend the iconographical and archaeological evidence, in his own writings, which contradicted his viewpoint.

One example will suffice. In Sayce's book, RACES OF THE OLD TESTAMENT, he wrote:

> The oldest attempt to construct what we may call an ethnographic chart—that made in the tomb of the Theban prince Rekhmal-Ra about a century before the birth of Moses—divides mankind into the Black Negro, the olive-colored Syrian, the red-skinned Egyptian, and the White Libyan. [55]

The only way that Sayce could believe that the biblical world is made up of Whites only, would be to disregard the first ethnographic table in history according to him. He said the table was produced one hundred years before Moses was born in Egypt. If Sayce can be trusted, racial distinctions were certainly in place at the time of Moses' birth. This will lend credence to the position that Moses' ethnographic table in Genesis chapter ten, reflected not only what he saw, but the Divine revelation he received as well. Based on Sayce's writings, Moses was born into a world where color diversity was already in place. Moses could have easily observed the dominant color traits of the sons of Ham, Shem, and Japheth and arranged his ethnographical accordingly.

After years of excavations in biblical lands, William F. Albright commented on Genesis chapter ten, "The Table of Nations remains an astonishingly accurate document." [56] How then could Moses' ethnographical table be inaccurate, considering he simply recorded from his observations and from Divine revelation? Yet Sayce and Albright will face the evidence and still make sweeping claims that the biblical world consisted only of Caucasians.

Our heart bleeds that men, such as Sayce and Albright (and they have legions of modern counterparts), would ignore the evidence and claim the biblical world was made up of only Whites. Dubois was frustrated with this kind of hypocrisy, inconsistency, and double standards fifty years ago! And we have not made much progress since. But this our friends must change as we enter the twenty-first century. Moses and the Holy Spirit certainly understood the words they wrote in Genesis better than any modern day scholar, including Sayce. We are certainly more willing to trust Moses' understanding of the ethnicity and racial classifications of the biblical world, than we are willing to trust modern-day scholar. In Sayce's book he maintained that "racial unity is determined by kinship in blood and physiological traits." [57] We agree with him. Why then would not Moses have observed the "physiological traits" and "kinship in blood" among the sons of Ham, Shem, and Japheth? Even after millenniums of inter-racial marriages between all three racial groups near the Equator Belt or The North Pole, it has not changed the basic complexion. The Table of Moses still remains "an astonishingly accurate document."

Scholarly and Eyewitness Testimonies

Scholarly and eyewitness testimonies also gives credence to the plausibility of a significant Black presence in Scripture. Let us "chauffeur" modern day scholars to the ancient scholars, in order to witness their eyewitness testimonies of the presence of Blacks in the biblical world. We will also include a few modern-era scholars.

A. In annotating the similarities between the Colchians of south-ern Russia, and the Egyptians, Herodotus made the following comments in his book called, THE HISTORIES, written before his death in 425 B.C.:

> ...it is undoubtedly a fact that the Colchians are of Egyptian descent. I noticed this myself before I heard anyone else mention it, and when it occurred to me I asked some questions both in Colchis and in Egypt, and found that the Colchians remembered the Egyptians more distinctly than the Egyptians remembered them...

> My own idea on the subject was based first on the fact that they have black skins and woolly hair...and...the fact that the Colchians, the Egyptians, and the Ethiopians are the only races from ancient times who practiced circumcision. [58]

According to the biographers of Herodotus, "As a young man he travelled widely--in Egypt, in Africa, and in other parts of the Greek world. He was born between 490 and 480 B.C. He died in 425 B.C." [59] His eyewitness testimony and insights provides us with treasurable insights into the ancient world. Herodotus further denoted:

> The Ethiopians...are said to be the tallest and best looking people in the world. Their laws and customs are peculiar to themselves, and the strangest is the method they have of choosing for their king the man who they judge to be the tallest and best-looking people in the world. [60]

In commenting on the ethnic makeup of Libya, Herodotus wrote the following:

> One other thing I can add about this country: so far as one knows, it is inhabited by four races, and four only, of which two are indig-enous and two not. The indigenous peoples are the Libyans and Ethiopians, the former occupying the northerly, the latter the more southerly, parts; the immigrants are Phoenicians and Greeks. [61]

Herodotus reported on two types of Ethiopians in Xerxes Army:

> The eastern Ethiopians--for there were two sorts of Ethiopians in the army--served with the Indians. These were just like the southern Ethiopians, except for their language and their hair: their hair is straight, while that of the Ethiopians in Libya is the crispest and curliest in the world. [62]

Modern anthropologist classify Asians and Indians to have extremely dark complexions, but with straight hair and therefore a part of the Caucasian race. Herodotus saw dark-skinned Asians and dark-skinned Africans as the same people racially only with different hair texture.

B. Pliny the Elder, or Pliny the Naturalist was a Roman author born of wealthy parentage in 23 A.D. Concerning the earlier history of Ethiopia, Pliny wrote that it was "a famous and powerful country as early as the time of the Trojan War when Memnon was its king." [63] He further observed that the legends connected with Cephus and Andromeda. He recorded that they were members of the royal house of Ethiopia, which indicated that the kingdom once "ruled over Syria and that its sway extended as far as the shores of our [Mediterranean] Sea." Isaiah 18:1-2 indicates at one time Ethiopia must have been a powerful expanding nation.

C. Diodorus of Sicily wrote:

The Ethiopians call themselves the first of all men and they cite proofs they consider evident. It is generally agreed that, born in a country and not having come from elsewhere, they must be judged indigenous. It is likely that located directly under the course of the sun, they sprang from earth before other men. Far, if the heat of the sun, combining with the humidity of the soil, produces life, those sites nearest the Equator must have produced living beings earlier than any others. [64]

D. Strabo the Geographer, was one of the most remarkable scholars of antiquity. A Greek geographer, born about 63 B.C., which qualifies him as another eyewitness to the biblical world stated, "The Syrians were Black, these being the Syrians who live outside the Taurus; and when I say Taurus, I am extending the name as far as the Amanus." [65]

E. Luke the physician recorded in the book of Acts:

Verse 1 - Now there were in the church that was at Antioch certain prophets and teachers; as Barnabas, and Simeon that was called Niger, and Lucius of Cyrene, and Manaen, which had been brought up with Herod the tetrarch, and Saul.

F. Josephus, the Jewish historian, wrote concerning the sons of Ham:

The children of Ham possessed the land from Syria and Amanus, and the mountains of Libanus, seizing upon all that was on its sea coast and as far as the ocean, and keeping it as their own.

...time has not at all hurt the name Chus; for the Ethiopians over which he reigned, are even at this day, both by themselves and by all men in Asia, called Cushites.

...Judadas, settled the Judadeans, a nation of western Ethiopians, and left them his name. [66]

G. Tacitus, a Roman historian who wrote concerning the origin of the Jews recollected the majority opinion of his day. He said the Jews were Ethiopians! After having mentioned several traditions regarding the origin of the Jews, Tacitus wrote:

The greatest part say they were those Ethiopians whom fear and hatred obliged to change their habitations, in the reign of King Cepheus. [67]

The Bible teaches that the Egyptians left Egypt a "mixed multitude" (Ex. 12:38). Perhaps, if Tacitus could speculate that the Jews were Ethiopians, this certainly suggests the possibility of a color component evident in the majority of the Jews. Sayce remarked about Jewish physical features: "The thickness or fullness of the lips again is a racial feature, characteristic of the African, and found also in the Egyptian and Jew." [68]

The Bible places the Hittites (Heth) in the family of Ham (Gen. 10:15). There is evidence linguistical, archaeological, anthropological, historical, and eyewitness evidence that each person mentioned in Genesis 10:6-20, in the family of Ham, would meet the American definition of a Negro.

NOTES
CHAPTER 6

1. Frank M. Snowden, Jr., Before Color Prejudice: The Ancient View of Blacks, Harvard University Press, Cambridge, MA, 1983, pp. 65-66.

2. George Wells Parker, The Children of the Sun, The Hamitic League of the World, 1918, quoted by Ernest C. Sargent III, Majestic Honor: Biblical Perspectives In Black History, Charity Church, Ft. Worth, TX, 1992, p. 32.

3. Anthony T. Evans, Are Blacks Spiritually Inferior to Whites?, Renaissance Productions, Inc., Wenonah, NJ, 1992, p. 34.

4. Ken Ham, "Science, Scripture, and Salvation," Radio Transcript No. 0207-932, "The Most-Asked Questions about Genesis," Institute for Creation Research, El Cajon, CA.

5. Ken Ham, Andrew Snelling, and Carl Wieland, The Answers Book: Detailed Answers at Layman's Level to 12 of the Most-Asked Questions on Creation/Evolution, Master Books, El Cajon, CA, rev. ed., May 1992, p. 143.

6. Ibid., p. 135.

7. Ibid., pp. 142, 145-148.

8. Ibid., p. 146.

9. Finis Jennings Dake, Dake's Annotated Reference Bible, Dake Bible Sales, Inc., Lawrenceville, GA, 1981, pp. 8,9,36,40, quoted by Cain Hope Felder, Stony the Road We Trod -African American Biblical Interpretation, Fortress Press, Minneapolis, MN, 1991, p. 132.

10. Ham, Snelling, Wieland, p. 146.

11. Salvatore Cherubini, La Nubie, Passage from Diodorus of Sicily, Collection l'Univers, Paris, 1847, pp. 2-3, quoted by Cheikh Anta Diop, The African Origin of Civilization: Myth or Reality. Translated from French by Mercer Cook, Lawrence Hill & Company, Westport, pp. 281-282.

12. W.E. Burghardt DuBois, The Negro, Oxford University Press, Inc., London, Oxford, New York, 1970, p. 12.

13. Ham, Snelling, Wieland, p. 144.

14. Ibid.

15. Ibid.

16. "Ham," The International Standard Bible Encyclopedia, Wm. B. Eerdmans Publishing Co., Grand Rapids, MI, 1956, Vol. II, p. 1324.

17. "Shem," Pictorial Bible Dictionary, The Southwestern Company, Nashville, TN, 1975, p. 783.

18. William Dwight McKissic, Sr., Beyond Roots: In Search of Blacks in the Bible, Renaissance Productions, Wenonah, 1990, pp. 16-17.

19. Ham, Snelling, Wieland, p. 141.

20. Martin R. Delany, The Origin of Races and Color, Black Classic Press, Baltimore, MD, 1991, p. 8.

21. Ibid., p. 9.

22. H.G. Wells, The Outline of History, Garden City Books, Garden City, New York, 1956, Vol. I and II Combined, p. 107.

23. A.H. Sayce, The Races of the Old Testament World, The Religious Tract Society, London and Tonbridge, 1925, pp. 38.

24. Delany, p. 9.

25. Ibid., p. 10.

26. Ibid., p. 11.

27. Ibid., p. 18.

28. Ibid., pp. 20, 21, 23.

29. Ibid., p. 23.

30. Ibid., p. 24.

31. Arthur C. Custance, Noah's Three Sons: Human History in Three Dimensions, Vol. 1, The Doorway Papers, Zondervan Publishing House, Grand Rapids, MI, 1975, pp. 148.

32. The International Standard Bible Encyclopaedia, p. 1324.

33. A. R. Fausset, Fausset's Bible Dictionary, Zondervan Publishing House, Grand Rapids, MI, 1977, pp. 268-269.

34. Ibid., pp. 186-187.

35. Diop, p. 7.

36. Charles S. Finch III, Echoes of the Old Darkland: Themes From the African Eden, Khenti, Inc., Decatur, Georgia, 1991, p. 134.

37. Martin Bernal, Black Athena: The Afroasiatic Roots of Classical Civilization, Vol. I, The Fabrication of Ancient Greece 1785-1985, Rutgers University Press, New Brunswick, NJ, 1987, p. 21.

38. A New Standard Bible Dictionary, Funk & Wagnalls, Co, New York and London, 1930, p. 234.

39. Josephus: Complete Works, translated by William Whiston, Kregel Publications, Grand Rapids, MI, 1960, p. 31.

40. Finch, p. 133.

41. Raymond H. Woolsey, "Men and Women of Color in the Bible," International Bible, Inc., Langley Park, MD, 1977, Special Section, p. 3, cited in The Holy Bible, Authorized King James Version, Heritage Edition, Stampley Enterprises, Inc., Charlotte, NC, 1977.

42. Sargent, pp. 11-12.

43. Custance, p. 103.

44. Alexander Hislop, The Two Babylons, Loizeaux Brothers, Neptune, NJ, 2nd ed. 1959, pp. 50, 34, 69.

45. Ibid., p. 69.

46. Dubois, pp. 12, 17, 18, 19.

47. Margaret Oliphant, The Atlas of the Ancient World: Charting the Great Civilizations of the Past, Simon & Schuster, New York, 1992, p. 59.

48. Ibid., p. 11.

49. "Shem," The Pictorial Bible Dictionary, p. 783.

50. Sayce, pp. 67-68.

51. Ibid., p. 238.

52. Martin Bernal, Black Athena: The Afroasiatic Roots of Classical Civilization, Vol. II, The Archaeological and Documentary Evidence, Rutgers University Press, New Brunswick, NJ, 1991, p. 262.

53. St. Clair Drake, Black Folk Here and There: An Essay in History and Anthropology, Center for Afro-American Studies, University of California, Los Angeles, 1987, Vol. 1, 3rd printing, 1991, p. 137.

54. Ibid.

55. Sayce, p. 36.

56. William F. Albright, Recent Discoveries in Bible Lands, Funk & Wagnalls Company, New York, 1936 and 1955, p. 30; a supplement in Analytical Concordance to the Bible, by Robert Young, Wm. B. Eerdmans Publishing Company, Grand Rapids, quoted by Woolsey, p. 8.

57. Sayce, p. 21.

58. Herodotus, p. 167.

59. Ibid., p. 1.

60. Ibid., p. 211.

61. Ibid., p. 336.

62. Ibid., p. 468.

63. Joseph E. Harris, ed., William Leo Hansberry African History Notebook, Vol. 2, Africa & Africans As Seen by Classical Writers, Howard University Press, Washington D.C., 1977, pp. 134, 139, 140.

64. Diop, p. 281.

65. Strabo, Geography, bk., 16.2, quoted by Ivan Van Sertima (ed.), Nile Valley Civilizations, Journal of African Civilizations, Rutgers University, New Brunswick, NJ, 1986, p. 219.

66. Josephus, p. 31.

67. Ibid., p. 653.

68. Sayce, p. 33.

Chapter 7

BLACKS IN CHURCH HISTORY: FACT OR FICTION

It has been our contention that the Black presence in Scripture is undeniably clear. It is unfortunate that so many have chosen to ignore the clear historical and biblical data supporting this thesis. We further maintain that the Black presence clearly continues beyond the biblical record and can be traced to significant contributions throughout church history. It should be of little surprise that if such data was neglected and ignored in the biblical record itself, then to continue that pattern in the analysis of post-biblical history is only natural. The pages of history reveals the extensive contributions of people of color; yet the River Lethe' has to some degree, successfully rinsed history's memory of these indispensable contributions. Where history has maintained these contributions, it has not credited them to those to whom the credit truly belongs; people of African descent.

It is our purpose, in this chapter, to examine some of the vital contributions to Christianity wrought by dark-skinned people. By looking at the strategic place Black African people have played in the history and development of the Christian faith, both through their piety and intellectual prowess exercised for the glory of God, we authenticate God's continual activity in the Black race. We also encourage Christians of African descent to see themselves as the continuation of a divine legacy. Our opulent heritage should serve to motivate us to continue dispensing God's truth by means of the talents He has deposited in our community; not only for the benefit of the Black community in particular but also for the Christian community at large.

Distinctions of Race

Before we can begin to discuss the issue of post biblical contributions made by Africans, it is necessary to review a brief history of North Africa and to define what is meant by the name "African." It is commonly known that some White citizens of the nation of South Africa, who are of European ancestry, consider themselves to be African. Although their definition may be a suitable definition in light of the geographic locale of their birthplace, our agenda is not limited to include such a definition. Although we certainly recognize the reality of racial intermingling on the continent of Africa, our central concern is people of color and the historical events that developed the various types and shades of people on the African continent who by today's standards would be considered "Black."

Throughout the course of the history of Africa, Egypt has served as the crossroads to and from the middle eastern world; Africa to the west, Asia to the east and Europe to the northwest across the Mediterranean. Egypt being the junction of the Mediterranean became the melting pot for both ideas and genetics. In addition to Egypt the rest of North Africa also served as an intersection to other parts of the world.

According to Diop, the original inhabitants of the region of North Africa were Black. However, three encroachments by cultures outside altered the appearance of dwellers in North Africa.[1] Around the sixth century, Arab armies made their entrance and forever altered the physical appearance and cultural environment of the population of both Egypt and North Africa. The success of the Arab invasions remain evident to this day in the faces and religious practices of North Africans spanning from Egypt to Morocco.

There were yet earlier entrances by peoples outside the continent of Africa. In the Punic Wars (four centuries prior to the Arabs) , Rome, the rising political and military force of southern Europe defeated Carthage, the great city of North Africa, and as a result began to colonize the African province for the Roman Empire.[2] It is significant to note that the Romans recognized the physical distinctiveness of Blacks in the Carthaginian army.[3] Even before the Romans prevailed over the Carthaginian armies, the Phoenicians had met with the natives of North Africa, not for the purpose of war but for the purpose of commerce. In spite of the Phoenician presence and racial intermingling, the Romans were able to detect an obvious Black presence.

The result of the "visitations" of the Phoenicians, the Romans and the Arabs all contributed to the lightening of the complexion of North Africans. By twentieth century standards, these light-skinned Blacks would still be considered Black in spite of cultural intermingling into their native genetic stock.

It is well established that although people belong to the same anthropological group, they are often dissimilar in physical features. For example, not all of the people of the Orient possess the same physical characteristics. Although there are obvious similarities between the Japanese and the Chinese, there are differences in their somatic type or physical form. It is much more common to see people of Chinese ancestry exceeding six feet in height; however, this tendency among the inhabitants of Japan is not as easily found. Both the Greek and the Nordic/Scandina-vian, for instance, are both Europeans and are classified in the anthropo-logical category of Caucasian; however, their features are noticeably different. Blue eyes and blonde hair are not the distinctives of a native of Athens. In the same way not all the people in the continent of Africa possess the same features nor are they all of the same somatic type. The Efik tribe of Nigeria differs in appearance from the tribesmen of the Sudan, yet both are African. The bottom line is that God has ordained the existence of a virtual cornucopia of permutations of skin color, hair texture, eye color and somatic type and the like. Often it is very difficult even for anthropologists to classify people groups in an appropriate racial category. This task is even further complicated when the unscientific eye addresses the issue of race. The reason that laymen may classify an individual as black, white or other is often not a matter of scientific assessment, but a matter of association, preferences and human reasoning.

For the Romans, the criteria of race was different from the criteria used by Westerners of the twentieth century. The Romans made a distinction between the 'swarthy' persons of North Africa and the inhabitants of the interior regions of Africa. In the nomenclature of the Romans the word Aethiops usually distinguished the person who was of Negroid physiognomy from the person simply with dark skin. Notably, the Roman use of the term Aethiops was not applied to describe all of the inhabitants of Africa. This leads us to question who in antiquity was not classified as Aethiops. It is possible, if not probable, that many of the great advancements of thought and technology wrought by North Africans might well be the intellectual progeny of those who would be deemed Black in our own milieu, but because of the Roman method of distinguishing race, history concealed the race of these great peoples or assumed them to be European.

Lloyd Thompson comments on the phenomenon of the Aethiops in the mind of the Romans.

> The 'problem' surrounding the presence of blacks in Roman society (in so far as it may be seen as a problem) was entirely one of Roman perceptions of the strangeness (sometimes not only somatic, but also cultural) of Atheiopes. The Roman concept Atheiops meant the black African somatic type, and it embraced all somatic appearances perceived by Romans as matching or very closely approximating to the image of the black African type as a combination of black skin, crinkly hair, thick lips, and flat nose which Romans carried about in their heads, but it was perceived as distinct from 'swarthy' and 'very swarthy' types (what we would describe as 'swarthy Caucasian' and 'Caucasian type' morphology combined with very dark skin), and even from types combining black skin with predominantly 'normal' (in our terms, 'Caucasian') morphology. In modern western societies children of mixed black and white parentage are invariably regarded as 'non white', and often there is also a tendency to accept as incon-

trovertible Madison Grant's dogmatic principle that 'the cross between a white man and a negro is a negro; the cross between a white man and a Hindu is a Hindu; the cross between any of the three European races and a Jew is a Jew.' But in the Roman perceptual context the progeny, let alone more distant descendants, of an Aethiops did not necessarily fall into the category of Aethiops: some where perceived as 'swarthy' (in our terms, 'swarthy Caucasian' and types of physiognomy combining black skin with 'Caucasian' morphology), some as 'white', and some as Aethiops, the classification in all cases depending entirely on the individual's physical appearance; there was no assumption inherent in the structures of the society that neither the black newcomer nor his descendants could 'ever become full members of the society because of the presence of the visible factor of colour' or shape. [4]

The point is that the Roman perception of who was "Black" and who was not differed substantially from the perceptions and notions about race and people groups in our own time. For instance, the Americas is home to a number of people of African descent with a mixed heritage. At this time in the United States there are no doubt few if any African Americans who are purely African without any Anglo or American Indian genetic interference. In spite of a very fair skin complexion in some African Americans, they are considered "Black", "Negro", etc., both from within the African American community and from without. To refer to an African American as "Black" is not necessarily a commentary on the individual's skin color. In fact the individuals somatic type, skin color, hair texture, and eye color could indeed be more akin to those of a Caucasian as opposed to Negroid, yet this person would still be considered an African American. In simpler terms "even though a person can look more White than Black that individual would be associated with the Black community. Contrary to our own perceptions here in the twentieth century, a Roman would consider the same person described above as having more Caucasian features than Negroid as more Roman/Caucasian than Aethiops (Black). Since the Romans used features other than skin color alone to distinguish differing peoples, it is easy to perceive how the inhabitants of North Africa could indeed be Black according to our modern understanding of racial distinctions.

Europe almost experienced a darkening effect in the same way that North Africa was lightened. In 732 A.D. Charles Martel halted the advancement of the Moorish armies of North Africa during the battle of Tours (France). If Martel's defense had failed, then the complexion of Europe could have been substantially different from what it is today. However, the Europeans of Spain were not able to arrest the advancement of the Moors. For this reason, deeper skin tones are commonly seen south of the Pyrennes Mountains.

In light of the cultural interchange that North Africa experienced and the ancient Roman perceptions of racial groups, in contrast to those perceptions in modern times, we must reconsider the fact that many of the contributors to Christian Theology who were native to North Africa were plausibly "Black" by our contemporary definition of the term.

The Church Fathers of Africa

For centuries church fathers, anointed men of erudition, have sculpted the development of the Christian faith and have postulated ways to articulate the deep and intricate truths of Christian theology. They have impacted the faith through their skill for rhetorical argumentation and consequently have thwarted many dangerous heresies by delineating the boundaries of orthodoxy. Earle Cairnes summarizes the significance of our ancient leaders when he said,

> The writings of the Fathers do much to fill the gap in historical knowledge between the New Testament period and the latter part of the fourth century. The leading men of the Church, by pen as well as by voice, formulated apologetic and polemical literature as they faced external persecution and internal heresy. Creeds were formed to give accurate statements of faith. Hence, the Fathers are of tremendous value in the study of the development of Christian life and thought in this period. [5]

Without their gift of keen insight and their desire for preserving the faith, Christianity would have surely endured several derailments.

Numbered among the Christian intelligentsia from antiquity were men of color who stemmed from African lineage; from dark-skinned peoples, namely the Copts, the Berbers and the like. One must be careful not to assume that the presence and genius of the church in Northern Africa or in Africa was solely of European development. As Diop points out, "Opposing the hypothesis that North Africa was inhabited from early Antiquity by a white race, we can invoke archeological and historical documents unanimously attesting that this region was always inhabited by Negroes." [6] From this we are to understand that in antiquity the Negro of North Africa was thought of as the `normal' inhabitant of North Africa rather than the exception. Armed with the idea of the prominence of the Negro in North Africa, we must readdress the notion that the Church Fathers of Africa Romana were only the offspring of Roman (Italian) colonists. The belief that they were Caucasian must be taken cum grano salis (with skepticism). The burden of proof is upon those who would make the African Church Fathers anything other than black, and not vice versa.

Tertullian

One candidate for the roll call of Blacks misplaced by history is the Church Father Tertullian. Quintus Septimius Florens Tertullian (c. 160 c. 225) was an African Church Father reared in Carthage as a pagan. Tertullian received a good education in literature and rhetoric. He was converted to Christianity some time prior to 197 A.D. St. Jerome says that he became a priest, but there are other indications that he remained a laymen. Eventually he joined the Montanist sect. The detailed chronology of his life and works has recently been much disputed.[7]

Tertullian's facility for rhetoric and argumentation impacted the religious environment of his day. In his PRESCRIPTIONS AGAINST THE HERETICS he argued that the heretics of his day had no right to refute the church and that Scriptures were the sole property of the Church [8]

Although many theological dictionaries and textbooks comment on the geographical origin of Tertullian as well as his illustrious career, the discussion of his ethnicity is in most cases not a matter of mention. One possible explanation for the lack of concern for his ethnicity in his own day, as mentioned previously, is the fact that skin color was not necessarily the watershed issue for determining race. In modern times, the assumption that Tertullian was "white" is natural for theological historians. This is to be expected from a Euro centric perspective. By referring to a Euro centric perspective we do not mean to imply that there was a conspiracy by White biblical scholars to suppress the contributions of dark skinned theologians (although that charge could be true of some scholars who centered themselves on racial pride instead of on scholarly propriety), but that they too may have been insensitive to the racial distinctions of the Romans.

Most African Americans can easily comprehend the many variations of skin color and physical types within the Negroid race as it is manifested in the Americas. Although different political circumstances may have created the mixed races along the southern coast of the Mediterranean, a similar phenomenon occurred in the western hemisphere. African Americans can easily claim Tertullian as part of their intellectual heritage, if not more easily than Europeans can make the claim. The affinity is not only the matter of skin color but the circumstances which created them.

Among Tertullian's greatest contributions to Christian theology was his contribution toward the foundation of the Trinitarian formula.

Tertullian argued against Calixtus, the bishop of Rome, whom he called "Praxeas."

According to Praxeas, the Father, the Son, and the Holy Ghost were simply three modes in which God appeared, so that God was sometimes Father, sometimes Son, and sometimes Holy Ghost-at least, this is what may be inferred from Tertullian's treatise. This is what has been called "patripassianism" (the doctrine that the Father suffered the passion) or "modalism" (the doctrine that the various persons of the Trinity are "modes" in which God appears".[9]

The theological beliefs of Praxeas made God into a schizophrenic Deity. Tertullian's fastidious zeal for theological propriety quelled Praxeas' faulty notion regarding the operation of the Godhead.

The treatise where Tertullian's legal mind shins is PRESCRIPTION AGAINST THE HERETICS. In the legal language of the time, a praescriptio could mean at least two things. It could be a legal argument presented before the case itself was begun, in order to show that the trial should not take place. If, even before the actual case was presented, one of the parties could show that the other had no right to sue, or that the suit was not properly drawn, or that the court had no jurisdiction, the trial could be canceled. But the same word had a different meaning when one spoke of a "long term prescription." This meant that if a party had been in undisputed possession of a property or of a right for a certain time, that possession became legal, even if at a later time another party claimed it.

Tertullian uses the term in both senses, as if it were a case of a suit between orthodox Christianity and the heretics. His aim is to show, not simply that the heretics are wrong, but rather that they do not even have the right to dispute with the church. To this end, he claims that Scriptures belong to the church. For several generations the church has used the Bible, and the heretics have not disputed its possession. Even though not all of Scripture belonged originally to the church, but now it does. Therefore, the heretics have no right to use the Bible. They are latecomers who seek to change and to use what legally belongs to the church.[10]

Tertullian was not the only benefactor to the Christian faith who hailed from North Africa. He was among many whose names are common in the discourse of theological history.

Saint Augustine

Without question, the most astute of theologians in the history of the Christian Church is St. Augustine. St. Augustine was born in 354 A.D. in the town of Tagaste in North Africa. The ORIGINAL AFRICAN HERITAGE STUDY BIBLE is specific concerning Augustine's life as a Christian theologian and an African:

> To this day Christian theologians reverently refer to the seminal works of Saint Augustine as among the most powerful texts of any time. Of the ninety books written during his lifetime, the CONFESSIONS and the CITY OF GOD are the best known. He is often called "The Father of Theology."

> Although history has tried to overshadow the fact of Augustine's African heritage, he was in fact of Nubian stock, educated at an African university and later ordained as bishop of the North African colony of Hippo. Augustine's mother, Monica, was raised in a Christian household, and she prayed fervently for the conversion of her husband, a former Roman infantryman, and her brilliant son. Augustine was an outstanding student at the University of Carthage, also free spirited and given to drinking and partying. [11]

Augustine's ancestry was of Berber stock. [12] The Berbers were a group of dark skinned people belonging to the vicinity of Carthage. Although Augustine's father was a Roman official and a pagan, one should not presume that his father was White European while Augustine's mother, Monica, seemed to be a native of Carthage. Although the Romans held the scepter of political jurisdiction over the population of North Africa, the dark-skinned inhabitants should not be thought of as minorities. In fact, quite the opposite was true, and remains true today with alterations caused by the sands of time.

> The present population of North Africa is predominantly of Berber descent, mixed with the invaders from Arabia who converted the country to Islam in the 7th century; and the negro slaves who were brought across the Sahara until the French occupation. But the proportion of black blood is small and almost exclusively confined to towns except in the Saharan oases, where the Berber race ...penetrated relatively late in recorded time. Such of the existing negro population as were not permanently displaced they enslaved; and to this day the oases are mostly cultivated for their nomadic Berber owners by a race of negroes, known as the Harratin, who provide their landlords with a part of their produce as rent. [13]

Thus, the amount of black blood in the Berbers of today represents but a modicum of the total ancestry. However, regardless of how small the percentage of black blood may be, yet it is present.

What we know of North Africa and its inhabitants before the fall of Carthage, when the Roman period begins, depends largely upon inference. There is no written Berber language and consequently no record of the Berber tribal kingdoms which existed outside the Carthaginian and Greek zones of influence. Ethnically speaking, according to Charles-André Julien (the best contemporary authority) "as far back in the past as the available evidence goes they (the Berbers) have never been a homogeneous race, anthropologically speaking; but a complex of races which neither the Phoenician penetration nor the Roman rule, nor the Vandal and Byzantine episodes nor even probably the invasions have greatly changed. The term "Berber" has really no sure anthropological base, but signifies certain well-defined linguistic and social characteristics. From the earliest times the Berber has always appeared, historically speaking as a distinct social personality, very marked, through and beyond the changing rulers of the Maghreb. [14]

Given the demographic climate of North Africa in the fourth century before the advent of the Arabs, to suggest that Augustine was a Berber would not be untenable nor is it inconceivable that this same area would produce more men of valor and renown. Nickerson records the story of one man of valor Septimius Severus, a Berber, who rose to the highest position in the Roman Empire.

Septimius Severus was born at Leptis Magna in Tripolitania in the year 146 A.D. of the Romanized ruling. He received a good education in his native province and adopted an official career as civil magistrate and military commander which took him to Rome. Eventually, after the murder of Marcus Aurelius' worthless son, Commodus, he won the support of the provincial Legions and made good his claim to the imperial throne. It was a claim which had no shadow of justification save the right of the strongest. He became Emperor by virtue of a military pronunciamento, but thanks to exceptional ability he was able to maintain his candidature against all rivals, and his reign (193-211 A.D.) marks the summit of Africa's importance under Roman rule. His unusually forceful personality has left many memorials, including numerous portraits. The triumphal arch commemorating one of his Easter campaigns still stands in Rome, and recent Italian excavations have revealed the magnificent monuments with which he endowed his native city of Leptis. [15]

Skin color was not an excuse nor an impediment for success at the time of Septimius Severus. The respect paid to Severus was indicative of the attention given to actual skill versus stereotypes. If Severus could be a Black emperor of Rome, then it should not surprise us to think that Augustin's father could have been both Black and Roman and that Augustine himself could also be the Black Father of Theology.

Augustine's trek to fame began when he moved from his native Tagaste to Carthage to attend school. Carthage brought some changes in Augustine's world view, namely a very undisciplined sense of morality.

> Augustine was some seventeen years old when he arrived at the great city that for centuries had been the political, economic, and cultural center of Latin-speaking Africa. Although he did not neglect his studies, he also set out to enjoy the many pleasures that the city offered. [16]

Prior to his conversion, one might consider the personal life of Augustine to be less than pious. Augustine's concubine bore him a son whom he named Adeodatus which means given by God.[17] It is this event and others similar to it (along with episodes of wandering through philosophical systems, such as Manicheism) which served as the premise for Augustine's conversion and concomitantly his cherished appreciation for the grace of God.

Many refer to Augustine as the "father of orthodox theology." The greater majority of his doctrinal opinions have stood the test of time and the scrutiny of many theologians throughout the annals of theological history. Few people are able to understand theology apart from life experience. In fact, the life and experience of Augustine were critical to his formulation of his views on sin and grace.

> Augustine's view of sin and grace was molded to some extent by his deep religious experiences, in which he passed through great spiritual struggles and finally emerged into the full light of the Gospel. He tells us in his Confessions that he wandered far from the path of morality and religion, sought escape in Manichaeism and almost fell into its snares, but finally turned to Christ. [18]

Upon observing his life experience through the lens of his CONFESSIONS, one can easily see his strong view of the grace of God. CONFESSIONS was a spiritual autobiography which chronicled the conversion of Augustine. González says of it, " It is unique in its genre in all ancient literature, and even to this day it witnesses to Augustine's profound psychological and intellectual insight." [19]

One of Augustine's greatest feats was his defense of orthodoxy in the Pelagian controversy. The theologian Pelagius placed emphasis on man's ability to initiate salvation. Augustine on the other hand maintains that salvation was solely a product of God's grace and apart from this grace man could in no way earn salvation. The thought and contribution of Augustine became the theological foundation for the Protestant Reformation as well as contemporary Reformed Calvinistic theology.

Athanasius of Alexandria

His enemies referred to him as the "black dwarf", [20] a comment that was not issued with the same sense of awe and appreciation as those who deemed Joe Louis "the brown bomber." The "black dwarf" was a derogatory term, but regardless of its derogation, it did not abate the colossal impact that this black man of small stature made upon theology.

The exact date of the birth of Athanasius is unknown, however, some suggests a date of ca. 276 . From all historical indications he was a man of humble upbringing among the Copts of Egypt.

> Since he spoke Coptic, the language of the original inhabitants of the area who had been successively conquered by the Greeks and the Romans, and his complexion was dark, like that of the Copts, it is very likely that he belonged to that group, and that therefore he was a member of the lower classes in Egypt. [21]

His class within Christianity was however among the highest. As a young man he served as secretary to Alexander Bishop of Alexandria. Upon the death of Alexander, it was made known to Athanasius that he had been chosen by Alexander to succeed him as Bishop of Alexandria. However, initially Athanasius withdrew in humility but later reconsidered and accepted the position. Athanasius' tenure as Bishop of Alexandria was somewhat tumultuous. His term was interrupted five times by the religious pressures of the Roman Emperors and political pressures from within the Church. Among the influences in Athanasius' early life was St. Anthony, also a Black Coptic monk, who Athanasius claims was the founder of Egyptian monasticism. It is said that Anthony was the child of wealthy parents. Anthony had planned to live off his inheritance until the gospel interrupted that vision of personal leisure. The story of the rich young ruler prompted Anthony to modify his life-plan as he found his own situation somewhat similar to the biblical character upon hearing the words, "If you would be perfect, go, sell what you possess and give to the poor, and you will have treasure in heaven" (Matt. 19:21). Anthony's conviction was to follow the prescription of the passage. He then dedicated his life to the cause of Christ and piety.

Both Anthony and Athanasius were involved in the theological war against Arius and the Arians. "What Arius taught was that the one who had come to us in Jesus Christ was not truly God, but a lesser being, a creature." [22] It was because of this heresy that the Council of Nicea met in the year 325 A.D.

Among the attendants of Nicea was the "black dwarf." Although he was not to be a major player at this Council (at the time he was in service to Alexander the Bishop of Alexandria as his secretary), his understanding of the theological conclusion drawn at Nicea helped him to defend orthodoxy thinking concerning the deity of Christ even with the threat of personal injury.

> The Nicene Creed insisted that God has fully come into human history in Jesus Christ. It sought to make this clear through certain key phrases in the creed: "That is, of the essence of the Father"; "True God from true God"; "Begotten, and not created"; "Of one essence [reality] with the Father." This last phrase was decisive, but it was the subject of considerable controversy. [23]

Athanasius exhibited an understanding of theological issues that was far beyond his own time.

> For Athanasius, the Word of God who rules the world is the living Logos of God-that is, the Word who is God himself. This view of God indicates that Athanasius, even before becoming involved in the Arian conflict, had developed an understanding of the Word that was different, not only from the Arians, but also from that view held by many earlier theologians. Before Athanasius there was a tendency to establish the distinction between the Father and the Word on the basis of that contrast between the absolute God and a subordinate deity. This was, Athanasius insisted, incompatible with Christian monotheism. [24]

The Letter of Athanasius C.E. 367

The letter of Athanasius written in year 367 A.D is critical to New Testament studies. The letter is significant in that it is the earliest evidence biblical scholars have for the inclusion of all twenty seven books of the New Testament. Eusebius (270-340), the church historian from Caesarea, had divided the works of the New Testament and some alleging themselves to be canonical into three groups. The *Homolegomena* represented the books that were generally accepted by all, including Hebrews, which Eusebius assigned to Paul. The *Antilegomena* were books disputed both for authorship and canonicity. The *Antilegomena* consisted of James, 2 Peter, Jude, 2 John and 3 John and Revelation. The third category consisted of those books that Eusebius deemed heretical and thus rejected them completely; they included the Gospel of Thomas, Acts of Andrew and John, and others.

Athanasius was the first church father to list all twenty seven books of the New Testament as canonical(that is, the collection of writings we know as the New Testament)! [25]

List of Early African Contributors to the Study of New Testament Textual Criticism

Below is a list of briefs on some of the lesser known contributors to the Christian faith by way of Africa. [26] In light of the evidence above concerning demographics of North Africa, this list of Church Fathers no doubt includes people of color who by the standards of their own culture may not have had attention drawn to their ethnicity due to their somatic type (cf. the arguments of Lloyd Thompson regarding the Roman view of race).

Cyprian, ca. 200/210-258. Thascius Caecilius Cyprianus, probably from Carthage, of a pagan family, baptized ca. 246, bishop of Carthage 248/249. Beheaded in 258 in the persecution under Valerian. The most influential writer of the Latin church before Ambrose and Augustine, since Tertullian was officially repudiated.

Facundus, mid-sixth century. Bishop of Hermiane in Africa.

Ferrandus, sixth century. Deacon in Carthage, student and biographer of Fulgentius.

Fulgentius of Ruspe, 467-533. Born in Telepte (Africa) of a senatorial family, first a procurator, then a monastic monk. Bishop of Ruspe ca. 507, in exile 508-515 and 517-523.

Liberatus, sixth century. Deacon in Carthage, wrote a history on heresies.

Macrobius, fourth century. Presbyter in Africa, and bishop of the Donatists in Rome.

Marius Mercator, fourth/fifth century. Probably African by birth, later in the eastern part of the Roman Empire, probably in Constantinople. Translated many writings from Greek.

(Gauis) Marius Victorinus (M Vict, Victorinus Rome, Marius), d. ca. 363. From Africa, a renowned teacher of rhetoric in Rome.

Became Christian late in life, giving up teaching in 362 (Edict of Emperor Julian). Wrote important commentaries on the Pauline letters.

Primasius, d. after 552. Bishop of Haddrumetum (Africa), author of a commentary on Revelation.

Quodvultdeus, d. ca. 453. Deacon, from ca. 437 bishop of Carthage, in 439 banished by Geiserich. Probable author of some sermons traditionally attributed to Augustine; the authorship of De promissionibus remains in question.

Tyconius, fourth century. From Africa, a Donatist, author of a commentary on Revelation preserved in fragments (mainly by Beatus).

Victor of Tunnana (Victor Tunis), sixth century. Bishop in Africa, died after 566 in exile in a monastery in Constantinople; author of "A World Chronicle."

Victor of Vita, fifth century. Bishop of Vita (Africa). Author of Historia Persecutionis Africanae Provinciae.

Vigilius of Thapsus, fifth century. Bishop of Thapsus in Africa, wrote against various heretical doctrines, probably died after 484.

It becomes obvious that the potential influence of men of color from Africa in the history of Christianity is significant.

Africa and the Sacred Writings

In any religion, what is considered the sacred writings of that religion represent the bedrock of that faith. Christianity is no exception in this regard. Apart from the Old and New Testaments our faith and doctrine would be little more than folklore. In every generation, people called by the name of God believed that preservation and transcription of the Sacred Writings have been essential to the vitality of the faith. II Kings 22 reveals the way spiritual renovation occurred within Israel when Hilkiah the high priest found the Book of Deuteronomy in the temple. Apparently, Israel's worship of the Lord had become so aberrant and adrift that the rediscovery of Deuteronomy was as a second genesis in the religious life of Israel.

"The king heard the words of the book of the law, he tore his robes. He gave these orders to Hilkiah the priest, Ahikam son of Shaphan, Acbor son of Micaiah, Shaphan the secretary and Asiah the king's attendant; "Go and inquire of the Lord for me and for the people and for all Judah about what is written in this book that has been found. Great is the Lord's anger that burns against us because our fathers have not obeyed the words of this book; they have not acted in accordance with all that is written there concerning us" (2 Kings 22:11-13).

The king, Josiah, realized Israel's severe disobedience toward God's laws and its requirements for a theocratic kingdom. The rediscovery of the "Book of the Law" alerted the king to the seriousness of Israel's spiritual state.

If the lack of the Scriptures caused such spiritual havoc in Israel, imagine the disarray that the Church may have suffered had the Diocletian persecutions of the fourth century obliterated the Scriptures. At the urging of one of his generals, Galerius, the Roman Emperor Diocletian issued an edict against Christians. "Even then, the purpose was not to kill Christians, but to remove them from positions of responsibility within the Empire. So, it was ordered that Christians be removed from every government position, and that all Christian buildings and books be destroyed."[27] It was thought that if the sacred Scriptures of Christianity could be destroyed, that Christianity itself would be destroyed as well.

North Africa and Egypt were amongst the hardest hit during the time of this ferocious brutalization of the Christian church. The historian Eusebius spoke of the tyranny, "All this [persecution] has been fulfilled in our day, when we saw with our own eyes our houses of worship thrown down from their elevation, [and] the sacred Scriptures of inspiration committed to the flames in the midst of the markets."[28]

Yet, through this most turbulent episode in the history of the Egyptian and North African Church, the oldest form of the Greek New Testament texts survived. Two factors account for this: First, brave Christians of 'the continent' risked their very lives to preserve the documents of the New Testament.

"In Abitina (in North Africa) the bishop handed over the Scriptures on demand. But his congregation disowned his act and carried on the church meeting in the home of the reader Emeritus. When the interrogators asked Emeritus to hand over his copies, he refused, saying he had 'the Scriptures engraved on his heart.'" [29]

Second, the dry and airy region of North Africa was a perfect vault in which to store the literary treasures of Scripture. [30] Africa made a considerable contribution to the security and preservation of the New Testament in the face of the most severe treatment in the Diocletian persecution. Somewhere in God's providence the Black African, be he Coptic, Ethiopian, Egyptian or other, was destined to participate in the preservation of the written Word of God. Bible readers today owe a debt of gratitude for these brave saints who kept alive the inscripted Word of God.

The history of the Coptic Church and its preservation of Scripture began early. The Coptic Church ascribes the advent of Christianity into Egypt to the preaching of St. Mark the Evangelist. Some in the scholarly community suggests that the first century (a necessary date if St. Mark were the herald for the gospel in Egypt) is much to early for the presence of Christianity in Egypt. Scott Moncrief in his book PAGANISM AND CHRISTIANITY in Egypt averred that a first century date for Christianity in Egypt had no historical support. He asserted that the third century was far more appropriate for the inception of the Christian faith into Egypt. To the contrary, J. M. Plumley stated,

> Now, while it is true to say that up to the present we do not possess any first hand evidence for the existence of Christianity in Egypt prior to the second half of the 2nd century; nevertheless, from indirect evidence it may be argued that it would seem probable that quite early in the second half of the 1st century some knowledge of the Christian faith had reached Egypt. It is significant that by 180 A.D., when the Church in Alexandria appears in the full daylight of history, it is a flourishing institution with an organization and school of higher learning attached, which must have already made its influence felt far beyond the city itself. It hardly seems that such was the result of a mushroom growth.[31]

For the most part, the accounts of the dawn of Christianity in Egypt are legendary. A fifth century document known as CODEX BEZAE CANTA-BRIGIENSIS, states that Apollos [of Acts 18] received his Christian training before leaving his home in Egypt. If this is true, then Christianity would have had a presence in Egypt at least by the mid 50's of the first century. Although some scholars strongly support a later date for Christianity in Egypt, a small scrap of papyri [the paper of the ancient Egyptian world] provides us with evidence to the contrary. One of the smallest yet invaluable fragments of New Testament Scripture is known as Papyri 52 [also known as the Ryland's Papyri]. The German scholar Ferdinand Christian Baur stated that the Gospel of John must have been written as late as AD 160. If this were true, then John, the apostle, could not possibly have been the author. But the discovery of Papyri 52, a small scrap of papyri of John 18 no larger than the palm of the average hand, completely refuted Baur's notions. Papyri 52 was dated circa AD 125 and it was very difficult to locate a copy of the Gospel of John almost 40 years after the recording of the original. The noted textual critic Bruce Metzger stated,

Although the extent of the verses preserved is so slight, in one respect this tiny scrap of papyrus possesses quite as much evidential value as would the complete codex [book]. Just as Robinson Crusoe, seeing but a single footprint in the sand, concluded that another human being, with two feet, was present on the island with him. P52 proves the existence and use of the Fourth Gospel during the first half of the second century in a provincial town along the Nile, far removed from its traditional place of composition (Ephesus in Asia Minor). Had this little fragment been known during the middle of the past century, that school of the New Testament criticism which was inspired by the brilliant Tübingen professor, Ferdinand Christian Baur, could not have argued that the Fourth Gospel was not composed until about the year 160. [32]

Since the papyrus was found in Egypt, the probability exists that there were Christians in Egypt as early as ca,. AD 125.[33] They would have then been strategically involved in the preservation of the sacred writings.

The Writings of Addai: The Legend of Abgar "the Black"

Although he was neither African by birth nor did he serve in Africa, to Addai, a fifth century Church Father from the east, is ascribed an apocryphal work penned in Syriac known as THE TEACHING OF ADDAI. In this work, Addai sought to expand the `earlier legendary correspondence between Jesus and Abgar V.' [34] In this legendary account, Abgar V, who served as king of Edessa about the same time that Christ walked the byways of Palestine, gave an invitation to Christ to come to the city of Edessa; however, Jesus decline to make the trip due to the urgency of His mission to Israel. A note of interest is that Addai appends to the name of Abgar the designation "the black" [hence, "Abgar the Black"]. The term "the black" was an indicator of Abgar's race. Apparently Abgar was the king of a city located in Asia Minor and was of African descent. Although it is likely that the account of the invitation is fiction, the characters are not fictional, neither Jesus nor Abgar "the Black."

The Ethiopic Church

Oral tradition is primarily the vehicle of the early history of the Black Ethiopic Church. Bruce Metzger stated:

"The time and circumstance of the planting of the Church in Ethiopia are difficult to ascertain. The account in Acts viii. 26-39 of the conversion by Philip of an Ethiopian who was chamberlain of the

Candace (or queen) of the Ethiopians is often assumed to have a bearing on the introduction of Christianity into Ethiopia." [35]

This assumption was held by early church witnesses such as Irenaeus (Adv. Haer . IV. xxiii. 2) and Eusebius (Hist. eccl . II. i. 13). [36] Other traditions affirm that other apostles evangelized Ethiopia. "Rufinus and Socrates report that Matthew preached in Ethiopia; Gelasios of Cyzicus links the name of Bartholomew with that country; and the confused account concerning the preaching of the apostles which is attributed to Epiphanius of Cyprus mentions Ethiopia in connection with the work of Andrew. [37] Although solid evidence for first century Christianity in Ethiopia was scarce, by the fourth century stronger signs appeared. However, it may be a bit hasty to say with surety that Christianity was not in Ethiopia prior to the fourth century. By the sixth century Cosmas Indicopleustes journeyed to Ethiopia and found it thoroughly Christianized.[38]

Ethiopia was considered a possible ally for the European Crusaders of the 11th, 12th and 13th centuries. If we are to assume a contiguous presence for Christianity in Ethiopia from the fourth century, by the time of the Crusades, Christianity would have been indigenous to Ethiopia for in excess of 900 years! Parts of the European theater were not successfully evangelized until the Charlemagne and the Carolingian Empire (ca. 9th century).

When news of the existence of Ethiopia reached European courts, there was hope for finding this [black] Christian kingdom and forming an alliance with it to launch a great crusade that would attack the Moslems from two different fronts. Unfortunately, the slave trade became the primary import of Africa to the European eye. [39]

Christianity in the Ethiopic tradition from centuries past has also left behind a witness to their reverence for the Scriptures. There are also several thousand manuscripts of the New Testament printed in Ethiopic. Most of these manuscripts are dated between sixteenth and seventeenth centuries. The presence of these documents indicate that Christianity must have thrived in Ethiopia about the same time that Martin Luther (1483-1546) and Huldrych Zwingili (1484 1531) wrote and taught in Germany. This reality belies the notion that slave traders brought Christianity to the African Continent. Christianity was thriving before they came.

To this day, the Christian faith remains a part of the vim and vitality of Ethiopia. The Ethiopians are well known for their pageantry, grandeur and pomp in the celebration of Easter and other Christian festivals.

Christianity in the Congo

In 1483 the Portugese were busily establishing alliances and
colonies on the African Coast. In 1483, an expedition landed at the mouth
of the Congo and it was learned that this land, and vast territories in the
interior of the continent, were ruled by the "Manicongo" [the chieftain].
Since they hoped to reach Ethiopia by sailing up the Congo, they treated
the Manicongo's subjects respectfully. Four Portuguese remained behind,
and four Africans were taken as guest to the court of Lisbon. When these
voyagers returned with stories of the wonders of European civilization, and
of their good treatment in Lisbon, the Manicongo decided to become an
ally of the Portuguese, who in turn sent missionaries and craftsmen. After
a month of Christian preaching, the Manicongo was baptized and took the
Christian name of Joao, after the king of Portugal. Portuguese military
support in wars against his neighbors convinced the Manicongo that he
had made the right choice.

The next Manicongo, Afonso, was even more favorable to the
Portuguese and their missionaries. In 1520, after long negotiations, Pope
Leo X consecrated Henrique, a brother of Afonso, as bishop of the Congo.
On his return to his land, however, the new bishop found that many
European clergymen paid little attention to his directives. He died in 1530,
and two years later the Congo was placed under the jurisdiction of the
Portuguese bishop of the nearby island of Sao Tome. [40]

Continuing the Legacy

There are many more chapters in the annals of history to be
written both by and about the Christians of African descent. If these
stories are to be scripted, the legacy must be continued by us today. Even
now the gospel message grows and flourishes on the continent of Africa.
Today is the day that Africa again has its turn to be the seed bed of Christianity, as Europe and North America have been now for centuries. At the
present time seminaries and Bible schools alike call for African American
missionaries to return to Africa to assist them in strengthening the foothold
of the gospel in Africa for the benefit of the world.

1. Cheik Anta Diop, The African Origin of Civilization: Myth or Reality, trans. by Mercer Cook, (Westport, CT: Lawrence Hill & Company, 1974), 65.

2. The Romans fought three Punic Wars against Carthage; First Punic War 264-241 B.C.E., Second Punic War 218-201 B.C.E., and Third Punic War 149-146 B.C.E.

3. Lloyd A. Thompson, Romans and Blacks, (Norman, OK: University of Oklahoma Press, 1989), 59.

4. Lloyd A. Thompson, Romans and Blacks, (Norman, OK: University of Oklahoma Press, 1989), 158, cites M. Banton, White and Coloured: The Behavior of British People Towards Coloured Immigrants, (London, 1959), 63-4, cf. 84, and E.J.B. Rose, Colour and Citizenship: A Report on British Race Relations, (Oxford, 1969), 14. His point is to demonstrate that skin color was not necessarily a designation of the negroid race in the mind of the Roman.

5. Earle Cairns, Christianity through the Centuries, (Grand Rapids: Zondervan, 1961), 75.

6. Cheik Anta Diop, The African Origin of Civilization: Myth or Reality, trans. by Mercer Cook, (Westport, CT: Lawrence Hill & Company, 1974), 65.

7. F. L. Cross, ed., The Oxford Dictionary of the Christian Church, (London: Oxford University Press, 1983), 1352.

8. Justo L. Gonzalez, The Story of Christianity, vol. 1, (San Francisco: Harper San Francisco, 1984), 74.

9. Ibid. 77.

10. Justo Gonzalez, The Story of Christianity, vol. 1, (San Francisco: Harper Collin, 1984), 74.

11. The Original African Heritage Study Bible, (Nashville, TN: The James Winston Publishing Company, 1993), 1831.

12. Keith Irvine, The Rise of the Colored Races, (New York: W. W. Norton & Company, 1970), 19.

13. Jane Soames Nickerson, A Short History of North Africa, (New York: Biblo and Tannen, 1968), 14.

14. Jane Soames Nickerson, A Short History of North Africa, (New York: Biblo and Tannen, 1968), 13-14.

15. Jane Soames Nickerson, A Short History of North Africa, (New York: Biblo and Tannen, 1968), 26.

16. Justo Gonzalez, The Story of Christianity, vol. 1, (San Francisco: Harper Collins, 1984), 208.

17. Ibid.

18. Louis Berkhof, The History of Christian Doctrines, (Grand Rapids: Baker, 1975), 131.

19. Justo L. Gonzalez, The Story of Christianity, vol. 1, (New York: Harper Collins, 1984), 215.

20. Justo Gonzalez, The Story of Christianity, vol. 1, (San Francisco: Harper Collin, 1984), 173.

21. Justo Gonzalez, The Story of Christianity, vol. 1, (San Francisco: Harper Collin, 1984), 173.

22. Ibid., 174.

23. John H. Leith, ed., Creeds of the Churches, (Louisville: John Knox Press, 1973), 29.

24. Walter Elwell, ed., Evangelical Dictionary of Theology, (Grand Rapids: Baker, 1984), 95.

25. The information above on the Eusebius canonical classifications and the Letter of Athanasius are taken from the © Unpublished Notes on New Testament Introduction, (1988) of Dr. Harold W. Hoehner, Professor of New Testament Studies, Dallas Theological Seminary.

26. The ensuing list of church fathers are provided by Kurt and Barbara Aland, The Text of the New Testament, (Grand Rapids: Eerdmans, 1987), 212-216.

27. Justo L. Gonzalez, The Story of Christianity, (San Francisco: Harper San Francisco, 1984), 104.

28. Philip Wesley Comfort, The Quest for the Original Text of the New Testament, (Grand Rapids: Baker, 1992), Ecclesiastical History 8:2:1, 13.

29. Philip Wesley Comfort, The Quest for the Original Text of the New Testament, (Grand Rapids: Baker, 1992), 15.

30. The humidity in Europe and other areas of the Mediterranean made those areas inhospitable for preventing the decay of the type of parchments and papyri used to script the first copies of the Sacred Scriptures for the New Testament.

31. J. M. Plumley, Palestine Exploration Quarterly, vol. 89, 1957, 70-81.

32. Bruce Metzger, The Text of the New Testament, (Oxford: Oxford University Press, 1968), 39.

33. Kurt and Barbara Aland, The Text of the New Testament, (Grand Rapids: Eerdmans, 1987), 196.

34. Kurt and Barbara Aland, The Text of the New Testament, (Grand Rapids: Eerdmans, 1987), 216.

35. Bruce Metzger, The Early Versions of the New Testament, (Oxford: Oxford University Press, 1977), 217.

36. Ibid.

37. Ibid.

38. Metzger cites Topographica Christiana, iii (Migne, PG lxxxviii,

col. 169), Eng. Trans. by J. W. McCrindle, (London, 1897), p. 120. as a reference to the comments of Cosmas Indicopleustes.

39. Justo L. Gonzalez, The Story of Christianity, vol. 1, (San Francisco: Harper San Francisco, 1984), 400.

40. Justo L. Gonzalez, The Story of Christianity, (San Francisco: Harper San Francisco, 1984), 402.

CONCLUSION

We hope we have clearly demonstrated that people of African descent have much to be proud of. Our roots are full of heroes who have made a wealth of contributions to the progress of mankind in general and the establishment and promotion of God's kingdom in particular. The pages of history are overflowing with the positive presence of Black people in God's redemptive story, a story which ought to be rehearsed over and over again.

With this knowledge, however, comes great responsibility. Knowing what we have accomplished in the past ought to influence what we do in the present and aspire to become in the future. We have no excuse for limiting our potential, or leaving to others the exclusive control of our own well-being. God has more than demonstrated that we are endowed with the tools necessary to maintain our families, develop our communities and shape our society. So confident was God in His creation of us that He entrusted to us a strategic role in developing civilizations, recording and preserving His inerrant Word, and expanding His kingdom in history. How then can we do less than give Him our best in reclaiming a generation who has left the "faith of our fathers."

It is our hope that this work has inspired you to become one of God's agents for change to help rebuild the walls of our community that have been destroyed by racism on one hand and apathy on the other. Only as we return to a biblically-based faith in God that is lived out daily can we ever hope to see things improve for us as a people. "God did not bring us this far to leave us," but it will take total submission to Him and His authority before we will see Him do for us today what He did through us yesterday.

Simply recognizing our Great heritage is not enough. God is not concerned with enlarging our egos but transforming our lives. Unless this knowledge causes us to submit to and glory in our God, then we will be a defeated and powerless people no matter what we accomplish. Our ultimate greatness then, whether individually or as a people, is not in our race but in our God, so that if there is anything worth boasting about, it has to be our relationship with Him -

Thus says the Lord, 'Let not a wise man boast of his wisdom, and let not the mighty man boast of his might, let not a rich man boast of his riches; but let him who boasts boast of this, that he understands and knows Me, that I am the Lord who exercises lovingkindness on earth; for I delight in these things,' declares the Lord'" (Jeremiah 9:23-24).

SELECTED BIBLIOGRAPHY

BOOKS BY BLACKS ON BLACKS IN THE BIBLE
AND THE ANCIENT WORLD

Dillard, William LaRue, Biblical Ancestry Voyage: Revealing Facts of Significant Black Characters, Aaron Press, Morristown, NJ, 1989.

Diop, Cheikh Anta, The African Origin of Civilization: Myth or Reality, ed. & translated by Mercer Cook, Lawrence Hill & Company, Westport, 1974.

Drake, St. Clair, Black Folk Here and There: An Essay in History and Anthropology, Vol. 1, Center for Afro-American Studies, University of California, Los Angeles, 1987, 3rd printing, 1991.

Drake, St. Clair, Black Folk Here and There: An Essay in History and Anthropology, Vol. 2, Center for Afro-American Studies, University of California, Los Angeles, 1990.

Edwards, Jefferson, Chosen...Not Cursed! - Destiny of the Spiritual Ethiopian, Vincom, Inc., Tulsa, OK, 1989.

Evans, Anthony T., Are Blacks Spiritually Inferior To Whites?: The Dispelling of an American Myth, Renaissance Productions, Inc., Wenonah, NJ, 1992.

Fowler, Jackie, My People Are Destroyed for Lack of Knowledge: A Biblical Account in Chart Form, Fowler Enterprises, Tulsa, OK, 1991.

Harris, Joseph E. (ed.), Pillars in Ethiopian History: The William Leo Hansberry African History Notebook, Vol. 1, Howard University Press, Washington, D.C., 1981.

Johnson, John L., The Black Biblical Heritage: Four Thousand Years of Black Biblical History, Winston-Derek Publishers, Inc., Nashville, TN, rev. ed. 1993.

McCray, Walter Arthur. The Black Presence in the Bible. Chicago: Black Light Fellowship, 1990.

The Black Presence in the Bible and the Table of Nations. Chicago: Black Light Fellowship, 1990.

McKissic, William Dwight, Sr. Beyond Roots: In Search of Blacks in the Bible. Wenonah, N.J.: Renaissance Productions, 1990.

Mosley, William, What Color Was Jesus?, African American Images, Chicago, 1987.

Perryman, Wayne, Thought Provoking Bible Studies of the 90's, Consultants Confidential, Mercer Island, Washington, 1992, reprinted 1993.

Snowden, Frank M., Jr., Before Color Prejudice: The Ancient View of Blacks, Harvard University Press, Cambridge, MA, 1983.

Snowden, Frank M., Jr., Blacks in Antiquity: Ethiopians in the Greco-Roman Experience, The Belknap Press of Harvard University Press, Cambridge, MA, 1970.

Van Sertima, Ivan, (ed.), Nile Valley Civilizations, Journal of African Civilizations, Rutgers University, New Brunswick, NJ, 1986.

Van Sertima and Rashidi, Runoko (ed.), African Presence in Early Asia, Transaction Books, New Brunswick, rev. ed. 1988.

Van Sertima (ed.), African Presence in Early Europe, Transaction Books, New Brunswick, 1985, 4th printing 1988.